THE POWER OF SHARING

the
power
of
sharing

stories of hope, love,
support, and healing
from **i understand**

edited by **Vonnie Woodrick**

WILLIAM B. EERDMANS PUBLISHING COMPANY

GRAND RAPIDS, MICHIGAN

Wm. B. Eerdmans Publishing Co.
4035 Park East Court SE, Grand Rapids, Michigan 49546
www.eerdmans.com

Book design by Lydia Hall

Printed in the United States of America

30 29 28 27 26 25 24   1 2 3 4 5 6 7

ISBN 978-0-8028-8446-6

Library of Congress Cataloging-in-Publication Data

A catalog record for this book is available from the Library of Congress.

*The stories in this book are dedicated
to everyone who is living in pain and
the people who support them.*

CONTENTS

Contents

TWO: STORIES OF LOVE

Contents

THREE: STORIES OF SUPPORT

Contents

FOUR: STORIES OF HEALING

FOREWORD

Depression is a disguise. It hides you from yourself with feelings of worthlessness that make you believe that you are weak or that you should be doing better, more, or differently than you are. It hides you from the people around you, trying to make you believe that you are unloved, that you are alone, and that no one would miss you if you were gone. It disguises your future, telling you that there is no hope, nothing to look forward to, and no better days ahead.

Unfortunately for me, I'd always understood depression as an "emotional disorder." In other words, my feelings were all messed up, and that meant that (1) I was responsible for getting them jumbled up in the first place; (2) I needed to figure out how to put them back the "right way"; (3) because I was different from "the right way," I must be an aberration and everyone else must be "normal"; (4) healing meant that I would completely cure the problem forever; and (5) if I couldn't figure out how to get myself mentally healthy, who would trust me again as a partner, as a professional, or even as a friend? As it turned out, the harder I worked at all of these things, the worse my depression got, which led me to blaming myself even more. What is wrong with me?

After all, what reason did I have to be depressed? I had a daughter and a wife I loved more than anything in the world. I had a career I could be proud of at a highly successful company my family built. I could go anywhere, do anything, buy whatever I wanted. What could I possibly be missing in my life that would lead to my feeling so unhappy, unfulfilled, and unable to cope with it all? If everything in life seemed to be going my way, but I still felt unhappy (I reasoned), it must mean that something was wrong with who I was as a person.

My first big breakthrough came when I learned that depression (and many related conditions) is best understood as an issue of brain health—not mental health or emotional health, despite the language usually used around these types of issues. In other words, the brain is an organ of the body, just like the kidneys, the heart, or the lungs. When something is wrong or broken with one of these, we treat the specific body part, but we don't disregard the entire person as a result. Once I understood that something was physically off in the way my brain worked—that my neuropathways were not wired properly like those of a healthy person—I realized that this was a health issue in the truest sense of the word. I wasn't broken or weak because I was struggling to break free from negative thinking—I was actually working with a body part that was not getting everything it requires to do its job properly.

This led to my second breakthrough: I couldn't fix myself on my own. Depression lies to you about you own brain, trying to make you believe that since your brain got you into this, your brain can get you out. I had been trying for years to force my brain to "get happier" and then beating myself up when that didn't work. You can't simply think your way to lower cholesterol and better heart health. People don't end up on dialysis because they didn't send enough positive, loving thoughts to their kidneys. I needed to let go of the notion that all I had to do was will myself to feel better and I instantly would. That's not how medicine works—not for the brain or any other organ. My therapist suggested I try an antidepressant that would help balance the chemicals and allow my brain to better receive and work with the hormones it needed to process thoughts and emotions more fully. With a little time, she explained, I would feel myself start to return to a baseline that was more manageable and sustainable.

This led directly to my third breakthrough: "You're not alone." As my doctor wrote out the prescription for an antidepressant, he explained that a lot of people, even people I probably knew, were on this same medication and that depression was far more common than I realized.

"It's nothing to be ashamed of," he added. For the next few weeks, I turned those words over and over in my head. *You're not alone. It's nothing to be ashamed of.* What if he was right? What if this really was far more common than I ever realized? And even more than that, what if it really does mean that something might be wrong with Doug-the-bones-brain-and-body but not with Doug-the-father-friend-husband-and-human? What if the problem is not in who I am but simply in the physical makeup of my physical form? How might that change the way I see myself, blame myself, and allow myself the room and grace to find healing?

As I allowed myself to accept these truths, I started to see more possibility around me. I started working with the organization i understand. I joined a walking group. I started a regular yoga practice. I found myself making better choices with my food and drinking less alcohol. My physical health began to improve as my brain health started to improve, which showed me that the illness really was linked to my physical body instead of just the squishy, hard-to-pin-down notion of emotional health. It also showed me that I was definitely doing the right thing in taking this as seriously, in terms of diagnosis and treatment, as I would any other disease.

But I also learned that healing isn't always a straightforward, one-and-done type of deal, which was my fourth breakthrough. After a few years of improvement, I had a recurrence. My depression came raging back, and once again I found myself held hostage by negative, unwelcome thoughts that seemed determined to keep me isolated, sad, and locked in self-destructive patterns. It was disheartening to feel that I had done all that work just to end up back (or worse than) where I started. But just because brain health doesn't follow a predictable pattern doesn't mean I have to live in fear of it. "Healing" just means making space for improvement, not eradicating the depression altogether. A friend recommended a new type of therapy that I had never heard of, and it worked wonders, but I still had challenges. Some friends and family suggested that I undergo behavioral therapy at a forty-five-day treatment center in Arizona to help me break out of old thought patterns and establish new, healthier ones. That helped too. But nothing is likely going to "cure" my depression, and I have learned to accept that. I am thankful for the medications and therapy I have received (and continue to receive). I am also grateful for the people who never gave up on me. This was my fifth breakthrough: No matter how alone I felt, I was never without a community, and they loved me enough to speak up when they were concerned—even if it was uncomfortable or unpleasant. I was loved, depression or not. And they wanted to make sure I knew it.

As I started opening up about my struggles and speaking openly without shame, my community grew. Suddenly, people I'd never met came up to me in public to thank me for sharing my story at brain-health events and for sponsoring media clips to highlight the importance of discussing these topics. I began to realize that my willingness to be honest and open about my challenges made people see me as normal and relatable. They saw that I was willing to be vulnerable rather than secretive, hiding behind a mask or a smile.

Thanks to the people in my life and the various treatments I have been fortunate enough to experience, I know that my brain health is not something I can cure, but it is something I can treat and control. I know that my life and my future are so much more than whatever my depression tries to tell me or define. And I know that love really does heal.

The stories in this book—written by women and men who have been touched by the message and mission of i understand—are similar to my own. Stories of struggle. Stories of loss. Stories of healing. Stories of helping. I hope they will help you in your journey of understanding.

Doug Meijer

INTRODUCTION

Vonnie Woodrick

After my husband lost his battle to depression, it took many years for me to overcome the stigma that revolved around his death. I struggled with the reality of my family's situation. I didn't want to talk about it. I was confused, devastated, and heartbroken. I thought suicide was something a crazy person did.

My husband wasn't crazy. He was kind, loving, and gentle; he made me laugh, and he made our kids laugh. He was a good husband and father, yet he suffered from debilitating anxiety and depression. I didn't know depression had a deadly effect—suicide. Suicide is perceived as a choice, but my husband didn't choose depression. Depression chose him, and my husband wasn't the first. I worry about my own kids and their kids, the fifth and sixth generations, as four generations in his family have experienced the loss and devastation attached to suicide.

I now truly understand the power of sharing your own story—the story that's behind the smile. The one that is often hidden or buried deep down. The one you're afraid will escape and be exposed.

I recall the first message I received after posting a video of me, sharing some of my story. I received a message that read: "Not only have you saved my life, but you have also saved my family the devastation of losing me. I always thought they would be better off without me. You helped me see that is not true."

Tears flowed after reading and processing the impact this one message had on me. This was the first day that I truly understood the importance and power of sharing my story. If you make a difference in even one person's life, your story is worth sharing. But chances are many more lives will be affected.

Everyone has a story, and everyone has someone who needs to hear it. The path may seem long and hard, but pain doesn't last forever. There is a light at the end of the tunnel that allows us to heal and grow. Sometimes, it may seem like a lifetime to see the light, but it's there if you're willing to look for it and, more importantly, accept it.

The purpose of the stories written in this book is to encourage readers to share their own journeys and to understand the power of unleashing their stories. When we begin to live out and share our truth, we start to free ourselves from the pain the past may hold on us.

Many will tell me, "You have courage," or "You are so strong," simply because I share the truth of my own life, good and bad. Why does it take so much willpower to share difficult and misunderstood truths? Why is the fear of judgment embedded in our being as we are taught to sweep things under the rug and be silent?

My hope is that you find comfort in knowing you are not alone. We all have stories, have experienced pain, have made poor choices, have been betrayed, have experienced grief and heartache, and have made tough choices in our lives; yet those experiences can give us strength, set us on a path we are meant to be on, and give us the ability to help others who live through similar experiences.

Speak up. Speak out. Share your story with a brave and honest face, because when you do, you may never know the difference it can make in someone else's life—or better yet, your own.

Every minute of every day is a gift. The gifts we recognize along the way, the people we encounter throughout our journey, lead us to where we are supposed to be.

We've just begun; our journey is clear. Our new journey started almost twenty years ago and will continue until we are witnesses to the necessary changes surrounding mental and brain health, suicide, and pain.

Change the conversation with us—view the definition petition and sign here: https://www.iunderstandloveheals.org/definition petition/.

The stories follow. While there are some storytellers who share how I, personally, have impacted them, this book is not intended to feed my ego. Rather, it is to show you how someone else's story can affect your own. If my stories have helped others, simply by my sharing them, I have a feeling that yours will too.

one
Stories of Hope

NEW HORIZONS

Living with Schizophrenia

Brandon Staglin

In September 1990, in Lafayette, California, twilight cooled the world outside my bedroom window. I gazed out at the autumn landscape, where I knew green leaves had begun to turn red, geese traversed the horizon, and college students like me had begun their fall semesters. I saw none of this. I was trapped within the bars of my thoughts and feelings, and that beautiful world was passing me by.

The psychotic break I had experienced two months before still reverberated in me, its horrors echoing louder with time. Why couldn't my mind feel like mine again? Dr. Levin's medications were supposed to quiet my bizarre fears and enable me to regain my identity. I sorely missed the person I once was, strong enough to reach for the stars, only a month before.

Would I ever return to Dartmouth College, to spend blissful hours in the company of my good friends? Would I ever again feel the fascination of grasping principles of engineering or of human and primate behavior? Would I ever return to Oakland Zoo, to watch the endearing chimpanzee family I had been studying that summer as a volunteer research assistant? The doubt felt crushing.

Now, the only thing that made consistent sense was the certainty that demons lurked behind every corner. They eagerly watched for me to make the slightest moral mistake so they could tear my soul from my body and spirit it to hell, where they would dance on it for the rest of eternity. I could hear them cackling when I almost made fatal errors such as stepping on a crack or eating too much at a meal. Day after lonely day, as my family, my doctor, and I fought for me to regrow into the young man we once knew and loved, I grew exhausted and desperate. I knew I couldn't handle this fight much longer.

But transcendent moments had sometimes appeared, and I had savored these. One afternoon spirits had visited me inside my body, escapees from the hell that I so feared, and nearly took over. But the force of my will had expelled them, and in that shining moment I could breathe freely again. I had never felt closer to heaven. Such moments gave me glimmers of hope.

What if I could die on one of these high notes? What if I could seize one of these heavenly moments and end my life—would I then spend eternity in heaven? Deep in my gloom, the idea made me catch my breath.

As I drifted in this reverie, the warm calm of that September evening slowed my breathing, and I knew it was time. As I had heard of elderly folks passing away quickly, heartbroken, when their spouses had died, I knew I could choose to go to sleep and not wake up. I retrieved my sleeping bag from my closet.

"Good night, Mom. Good night, Dad. Good night, Shannon," I called toward the kitchen, a lump in my throat. "I'm gonna go sleep out on the lawn again tonight."

"Okay, Brandon," my mother replied, frowning. "Be sure to come in if you get cold."

I closed the front door and strode out to the lawn. As I spread my sleeping bag across the fragrant grass, my thoughts began to race. *Do I really want to do this?* I knelt. *Isn't there some reason to go on?*

I nestled into the cozy folds of the bag and gazed up at the stars. The galaxy's glow, once a solace and source of inspiration, now glared down at me. Lying there alone, I feared my dreams were dead. But the fresh scent of the green grass stirred my curiosity for life.

Yes! All that summer there had been a spectacle I wanted to see. As I had read about in Jane Goodall's books, male chimps would sometimes erupt into a ritual called the *dominance display*, bellowing, beating their chest, shaking branches, throwing stones, and charging headlong at their foes. This was exactly the kind of ferocity with which I wanted to take on my life. How thrilled I would be to watch a dominance display firsthand!

I decided that I would return to the zoo the very next day to see what I could see. This world, this universe, held endless potential for beautiful discovery. I renewed my vow to keep learning and grow-ing, and never to let senseless delusions crush my quest to find sense in the mysterious frontier we call life. Someday, I thought, I would fulfill my ambitions to literally reach for the stars through spacecraft engineering. My life had begun again.

Over the next six months, recovery was like climbing a slippery slope: two steps forward, one back. A day came when depression nearly overtook me again. I had tried so many medications, and my mind still felt light-years away. Maybe treatment was futile. Maybe I would never escape this vortex of frustration.

I developed a habit of shuffling aimlessly around the house—it felt better than sitting still with my thoughts. One Saturday morning I wandered into the kitchen. My dad was there, eating breakfast, but I barely noticed him. I stopped and stared at the floorboards in private pain, closed my eyes, and started to sway. That's when I heard my dad say something to me that was deeper than anything I had heard him say before.

"There is a lot of love coming from here, Brandon."

I paused for a moment and opened my eyes to see him gazing at me from across the counter with deep concern. In the steadiness of his gaze, I knew that he meant it. It felt like a far cry from our now-routine conversations in which he constantly reminded me to take my medicine. Moreover, it was the most profound thing about love he had ever said to me. Subliminally, I understood that my experi-ence and my illness had impacted him deeply. I felt at once embar-rassed that my weakness had hurt him and relieved that he loved me anyway.

It hit me that I hadn't felt love for a long time. I was too wrapped up in worrying about myself to reach that kind of connection. In that moment, I longed to feel and return that love, to feel and be a part of my family again.

I thought, *Okay, this is it. I remember not long ago the warmth of Sunday afternoon outings spent with my parents and sister. I will experience that again. I will get well again, for me and for them.*

That morning saw the beginning of love becoming a primary value in my life. My recognition of the primacy of love to give meaning to life gave me strength to keep pursuing my recovery.

On that day I dedicated myself to following my medicine regime rigorously because of what it could do. I set alarms on my watch to beep every six hours to remind me to take my meds, and I looked forward to appointments with my psychiatrist to go over how well my meds had worked each week. With each week that the voices had quieted and the world around me had gotten clearer, we celebrated together with high fives.

It worked. Three years later, I graduated from college with degrees with honors in engineering sciences and, of course, anthropology. I went to work at a spacecraft engineering firm in the Silicon Valley. I loved the work and applied to Stanford and MIT to pursue a master of engineering degree. When I received thick acceptance letters from both, I gripped them with joy. I was on track to fulfill my teenage dream. Feeling invincible, I decided to reduce my medication dose so I could sleep less and do better in school. I held on tight to the belief that my years of schizophrenia were behind me. Surely, it was not too good to be true.

Then, weeks before I was to leave for MIT, a relapse struck. My symptoms came crashing back. My mind tightened with anxiety. When my roommates found me one afternoon frantically kicking a soccer ball against the walls of our shared yard, muttering below my breath, they told me I was a worthless lunatic, and I knew something had gone truly wrong again. I despondently canceled MIT, resigned from my work, and, with my family's help, checked into a psychiatric hospital.

My second recovery was even harder. As months turned into years, I moved back in with my parents in their Napa Valley home. Though I could live in comfort from day to day, I lived in isolation and could not feel motivated to work. Life felt like the aimless drives I often took through the countryside, seeking and not finding meaning, and always ending up back at home. I wondered if my life was on course for another dead end.

But thanks again to my parents, and the nonprofit they had founded, One Mind, I found the opportunity to participate in a clinical trial of a new, neuroplasticity-based treatment: cognitive training. This trial, conducted by Dr. Sophia Vinogradov, punctuated the dawn of digital therapies, and I felt excited to be there at the beginning. Hope sprung up anew. I dedicated myself to the laptop-based brain-training challenges, and as each week passed, I found that it strengthened my focus, my social fluency, and my sense of purpose.

When the training was done, I had relearned the conviction that I could make a difference in my own life. Armed with confidence, within six months I was spending time with friends again and ready to return to work. Science had done me a favor, and I knew I would return it.

Still, before I could ultimately dedicate my life toward healing others, I had to grow beyond enthusiasm for science and caring for my family to caring for people, period. Fortunately, as a change in my medication made possible, my feelings were beginning to wake up and stretch.

That summer was pivotal. I had taught myself web development and was now working as a webmaster for my family's winery. As another harvest season approached in the Napa Valley, preparations for the Tenth Annual Music Festival for Brain Health were in high gear. My parents had hosted these festivals since 1995, raising money to fund research for more effective treatments, preventions, and cures for psychiatric illness. While the community was excited for the gala event, the impending spectacle had me on edge.

That day, I wished my parents had never founded this event. *Clearly*, I thought, *the whole festival and the organization it supports are inspired by my sickness.* I did not want to be a center of attention, especially when I had done nothing to deserve it. Since the devastating setback of my relapse, I still felt like a shadow of who I had been.

Now I had agreed to present myself as a poster boy for the festival's publicity. My mom and dad had made a choice when they launched the first music festival, and there was no turning back. *They chose research fundraising as more important than protecting my feelings.* I winced as I considered how selfish my own thinking felt.

As I dropped into my office chair that August morning, I opened my email to find an article about a family friend who was one of the music festival's biggest donors, Liz Browning, and her son Marc. Marc, I read, had schizophrenia and, after an encouraging recovery, decided that he was well enough not to need any more medication. This sounded familiar!

Tragically, Marc's relapse had left him near oblivion. When Liz eventually found him in his apartment, his condition had deteriorated seemingly past the point of no return. As the article made clear, Marc was just one young person among thousands of underserved young people, slipping away.

As I read Marc's story, the gritting of my teeth made my jaws ache. How could this injustice happen? Though the healthcare system had helped me, it was failing to come through for so many others. Suffering was an epidemic. What could I do about this?

Wait—I had a story of my own! Could I share my story publicly to build hope for the way the mental-health system should work? Could I use my story to support my family's organization, to enhance the research that could someday help young people like Marc to recover as I had?

I gasped in a sudden smile. I could see then that this work was not about me. Sharing my story was no longer about me. It was foremost about using my experience as a platform toward healing people in need—friends and their families. Nothing was more important than seizing this chance to pay it forward.

I picked up the phone. "Mom, it's Brandon. You know what the music festival needs? A website. I'd like to build one for it. I'll feature stories on the entertainers, the donors, and the incredible discoveries our scientists are making. And I'll use it to share my story. Our story. I can do this. What do you say?"

Within a month, the first website of the Music Festival for Brain Health was live. That September, hearing festival guests' praise for it made me swell with pride. In that moment, knowing that I had contributed to the event's success made me feel like a conquering, alpha chimpanzee, fresh off a dominance display. For the first time, I closed my eyes and prayed in thanks for my health and for the chance to be a part of a cause so crucial.

Today, I am president of my parents' organization, One Mind, and beyond proud to lead an amazing team to accelerate brain health for all. One Mind accelerates collaborative brain-health research and advocacy to empower all individuals facing brain-health challenges to build healthy, productive lives. Serving as president, with responsibility for the welfare of my team and organization, has necessitated my sacrificing the carefree time I once enjoyed, but the satisfaction of the work is more than worth it. This is only the beginning!

I sincerely believe that if all young people facing serious psychiatric illness could access care similar to what I received, they would have a splendid shot at recovery. Care that employs state-of-the-art medicine, engages the patient's agency, and rallies the support of their families can enable youth at risk to build meaningful, productive lives. I commit myself to ensuring that all young people at risk have access to such gold-standard care, in the name of healthy lives and a healthy world.

EMBRACING IMPERFECTIONS

Living with Feelings of Inadequacy

Shandy Longcore

I was born in April 1981 to a loving set of parents and an older brother who was—let's face it—as kind as an older brother can be to his kid sister! I grew up in Michigan in the Kalkaska area not far from Traverse City. My dad, Randy, was a jack-of-all-trades who started out as a teacher but ended up owning the town hardware store. My mother, Sheila, had a background in nursing and worked in management at the local hospital. I was a small-town kid living in a small-town world where I could walk practically everywhere, and this was during a time when you didn't worry much about where your kids went or how long they stayed out. Everyone knew where everyone else lived, and they probably knew a little too much about their neighbors, right down to whose family owned which dog.

Maybe you grew up in a place like that too. But what you probably didn't endure were feelings of inadequacy at the age of ten, at least as severe as those I experienced. That's not to say I was neglected or abused, or that my parents made my brother and me suffer in any way. If I could paint you a picture of growing up in that era, it would include making forts outside, playing ball with other neighborhood kids, and going on great vacations with my family to visit cities all across the United States. My dad lovingly referred to me as "Shandy Pandy," and by all accounts, I was destined to grow up as a pretty normal kid with a fairly promising future.

Looking back, I initially considered that I was simply overobsessing about my appearance. But what I know now is that I was actually suffering from some form of mental illness that met its match: *a really bad day*. What else could explain August 23, 1991, when I was just ten years old?

It was a rainy Friday, with a high of seventy-five degrees. The first day of school was still a few days off, and I'd had a pretty uneventful summer, certainly nothing to complain about. Still, for some inexplicable reason at the time, I somehow felt unloved, *even though I was completely loved*. In addition to those feelings I was a very impulsive kid, and I was likely suffering from an undetected mental-health issue. In my adolescent mind, I actually thought that if I could just cut off my hair, my mom would buy me a wig, and that would make me pretty. I took a pair of scissors and chopped off most of my hair before going to bed.

When I awoke with every intention of going to my mom to make it all right, I discovered that she'd left early for work that day. My father was also already at work and wondering why I wasn't on time to perform my duties alongside him that summer morning at the hardware store. See, when you own a family business in a small town like Kalkaska, your summers aren't exactly spent hanging around the country-club pool. For me, summer meant working part-time at the cash register. And when my dad came home to see what I was up to, his first words were something like *"What in the world did you do to your hair?"* and it went downhill from there. Instead of securing a chance to become pretty, I ended up in an argument with my dad. He returned to work still fuming over what I'd done, and I was left alone to ponder my next move.

Unfortunately, I chose the wrong one.

Years earlier, after our grandfather passed away, his 30-30 hunting rifle was handed down to my brother. I knew exactly where it was stored in the basement, and unfortunately it was not locked up. If you don't know anything about this sort of hunting rifle, here are the basics: A bullet fired from it travels nearly 2,400 feet per second, or almost half a mile, in the blink of an eye. At close range, it takes a bullet traveling at that speed just over one one-hundredth of a second to find its mark. All this is to say that if I pulled the trigger, there was no turning back.

Somehow, I loaded that gun and turned it so the barrel pointed directly at my chest. The last thing I remember before pulling the trigger is that I was unsure which side my heart was on. At the last second, thinking it was more beneath my right breast than my left, I shifted the rifle to my right. And then I fired it.

At this point, I need to be very emphatic. I do not want anyone to ever accuse me of glorifying that moment. Dramatic as it was—and largely the reason I'm writing this today—I would give anything to erase that split second in time. Because what happened next was not only the most trauma I hope to ever endure, but I think back time and time again to try to comprehend the intense and unspeakable pain that I subjected my family and friends to.

In the movies, they typically show a person catapulted backward by the force of a gunshot. Not in my case. I fell forward, and I can still see myself going down and realizing in a blur, *I'm still here*. Immediately, it was difficult to breathe, and I went in and out of consciousness, thinking to myself these words: *What have I done?*

More than anything else in the immediate aftermath of having fired a rifle into my chest, all I could think about was how much *I wanted to live*. My misunderstanding of basic anatomy at the time ended up saving me, because if I'd aimed the gun just inches more to my left, I would have shattered my heart and likely died instantly. Instead, I was in a position now where my natural survival instincts were taking over, and I remember somehow making it to the phone in the basement and trying to call my mom's place of work, the hospital. I managed to dial the first three numbers—2, 5, and 8—but I couldn't breathe. And there was a lot of blood. I slumped to the floor. And that's when my hero showed up.

For some reason I can only call a miracle, my mother decided to come home early from work that day. She found me dying on our basement floor, and rather than losing it altogether, she went into nurse mode. She grabbed beach towels to stanch the loss of blood and then made two quick phone calls, the first one to my dad, whom she realized would be able to speed home and take us to the hospital faster than calling for an ambulance. Then she called the hospital to report that she was bringing in a victim of a GSW, short for a "gunshot wound"—her own daughter.

My dad scooped me up in his arms, cradling me while my mom drove our Olds Cutlass sedan. Everyone in ER knew me, because they knew my mom, and now they were trying to save one of their best friend's daughters. I was told later that it was like watching a team of horrified technicians work feverishly on their own child.

I remember bright lights, people rushing to and fro, instruments and tubes, and people yelling. I knew some of them by name. I recall their faces coming in and out of focus, and in the next instant they were readying me for the Aero Med helicopter, bound for Traverse City. I felt so cold, and somewhere in the midst of all that chaos, I was repeating two words: "I'm sorry."

The bullet that was meant to kill me passed entirely through my chest, out my shoulder, went up through the kitchen floor, then finally lodged itself in the door of our refrigerator. Even though I missed my heart, I came very close to not making it. That day, I nearly wrote history so that there would be one less fifth grader in class that coming year and, for the rest of their lives, my parents would have only photographs and memories to hang on to of a lonely little ten-year-old girl whom they had tried to save but couldn't.

Had I not survived, they would have had to somehow go on for the rest of their lives wondering what had gone wrong. What could they have done differently? And my poor dad would have had to muster on somehow with the knowledge that we'd parted that morning on less-than-loving terms.

Who knows how my mom and dad would have endured every future birthday? The Christmases to come? Vacations now with only their son, and no one else in the back seat to keep him company? They would have had to wonder: What would I have looked like in my high school graduation picture some seven years later? Who and what might I have become? Would I have married, had kids, contributed to my community, chipped in on a world craving doers and helpers?

But instead of succumbing and being carried to the cemetery in a casket, with my father, mother, and brother grieving something they never saw coming, by the grace of God I pulled through. And I'm here, now.

I was in the hospital for two weeks, getting infusions of blood and enduring a tube in my lung and fighting against the onset of infection. The doctors and nurses were great at fixing my physical needs, but there was a missing link in my mental and emotional needs.

My friends and family came to visit me or sent expressions of love, while I came to realize that even at ten years old—perhaps *especially* at ten years old—I mattered. I counted. And I was going to get a second chance at life. What I was going to do with that power, I didn't know yet, but I was given the chance to figure it out. I learned how truly loved I was and that having a different head of hair didn't matter in the least. The local paper called it an accidental shooting, and we all let it go at that for a long time.

But I know better now. In fact, I've decided to dedicate this part of my life to rewriting that story. And I'm sharing this today because I want you to become part of that story, of the truth, and of my future.

I want us all to use our collective power to tear down the stigmas that surround mental health, just like i understand is working so hard to do. Why is it so easy for us to say, "I'm physically ill. I have the flu. I need help," but we hide in a dark corner and refuse to use the same voice to say, "I'm mentally ill. I feel like I might hurt myself. I need help"?

I'm not afraid to say that I tried to kill myself, and for the last thirty-one years, I've been trying in ways both subtle and profound to make up for that near-fatal mistake. I came to understand and believe in what I call the "Power of One." What a difference one person can make, the influence one person can have.

Just one person can affect the tilt of the earth for someone else. In the aftermath of my episode, I found power in "ones" like Mrs. Dalton and Ms. Balloo, Coach Henderson and Coach Dalton, Mom and Pastor Riley, my beloved best friend Becky, and many friends and family who invested in me. They all lifted me up on my journey of discovering and creating who I wanted to be. They asked me about my faith. They connected with me frequently. They encouraged me to get involved and to try new things, including sports, which became my main outlet. I found that exercise and meditation were coping skills that fostered healing and growth. Also, my parents took the time to research and understand my love language and how I interpreted love. So many angels helped me, but *one* at a time.

Starting as a young adult, I enlisted the aid of a counselor, putting aside what were long-term prejudices, and discovering that working with a professional listener is life-affirming and worth every minute and every dime.

I was challenged to embrace my vulnerability, my fallibility, my inability to control everything. In the process, I discovered how to accept *all* of myself and realized that nobody gets through this chaotic world without bearing blemishes and developing scars.

The difference between caving in to blemishes and scars and living with them can be expressed in one powerful word: *hope*. Because I chose to lean on hope, I didn't die after pulling that trigger when I was a very confused ten-year-old kid. That kid went on to have a successful high school and college career academically, athletically, and socially. I ended up as the director of a premier fitness club in the area, a position awarded to me at the tender age of just twenty-five, which, frankly, I thought was crazy of them. But they saw something in me. Now, I've transitioned to the work of sharing my story in hopes of cultivating *a whole new kind of team*.

Let me stress that I begin each day recalling a saying attributed to Mother Teresa: "If you want to make a difference in this world, start by going home and loving your family."* See, I have an amazing

---

* This quotation paraphrases remarks that Mother Teresa made in her 1984 Nobel Prize acceptance speech.

husband, Bill, and two very special twin boys, Brennan and Cameron, and I can't imagine this second lease on life that I have without them. We wouldn't be the family we are today if the barrel of that rifle had been just a couple of inches off. If my mother hadn't come home early. Had I not had such superior medical care. And had God not turned me into a miracle.

My time with you, on this page, has a theme to it, the power of one. It depends on the kindness of others, but also demands that you engage in conversation about what's bothering you. Whether you're the one hurting or the one actively willing to listen, it begins with two simple words: "Let's talk." If you're scared or hurting tonight, and you've been craving the moment, this is the time to stop being afraid and begin moving forward. . . . "Let's talk."

I'm grateful that you read my story. I'm grateful for the gift you are to your family and your community. And I'm grateful to know that you took the time to consider my words and might pocket something of what I've shared in this writing. I hope that you are ready and willing to reach out to a world of people who depend on you and me for better tomorrows.

I'll leave you with one final thought:

Hope is a *force* designed to overcome. Hope is already inside you. It's always at work. And hope is whispering to you even now. Let it drench you with its grace.

And to those of you who are navigating difficult times, know this:

I'm *here* to tell you that you are loved, even if you don't feel it.

I'm *here* to tell you that you do have a purpose, even if you can't yet visualize it.

I'm *here* to tell you that you were given this life for a reason, even if you can't grasp all the details.

Fight to figure that out, because it will be worth the struggle.

Inside every one of our giving and healing hearts lives the Power of One.

BROKEN LIKE ME

Living with Suicidal Thoughts

Joseph Reid

Mental illness has been a struggle for me for as long as I can remember. By second grade I was already feeling like an outsider. I never thought I was good enough to have friends or be loved, so I tried to win kids over by impressing them. I remember bringing in to school one day a plastic CHiPs helicopter with a working propeller and manually operated winch. I just wanted someone to pay attention to me. According to my understanding of the unwritten natural laws of elementary school, I figured if I had cool toys, I'd have friends. I quickly found out that that's not how the world works.

Second grade is about the time I developed the nervous habit of picking my nose—not just your standard, run-of-the-mill picking, either. Watching me, you'd think I was training for an Olympic medal. I was a serious nasal excavator. Don't get me wrong—I'm not an idiot. I didn't wake up one day and think, *Oh, the other kids didn't think much of my toys. I know what will impress them for sure! Nose-picking. Now there's an idea!* Nope. That's not how it went down. This wasn't something I was proud of. And admitting it to you today is not easy.

Far be it from me to do things halfway and leave my embarrassment isolated to simple nose-picking, I somehow developed the habit of eating my boogers too. I tried to hide my picking habit. I actually think that might be why I started eating boogers in the first place—it was a safe place to destroy the evidence. Well, if cool toys

21

didn't work, and digging for gold in my nose wasn't effective, why not go the whole ten yards and eat the little nose nuggets? I didn't know this at the time, but this habit was directly linked to my anxiety. And in elementary school, I was anxious a lot! A lot of anxiety equals picking a lot of boogers, which equals a lot of booger-biting. Do the math. Add them all together, and what do you get? A new nickname is what I got. My name was forever changed in the annals of my elementary school from Joseph Reid to Joe-Booger.

I think about this label now and then and am kind of blown away by how used to it I'd been. Kids would run away screaming when they saw me on the playground. "Ewe, Joe-Booger is coming! Hurry before he touches us with his boogers." It was 1983 when my second-grade teacher (a saint if ever there was one), Ms. Payne, sat down with my parents to let them know something was up and that she was concerned.

So, why am I telling you all this? I understand that going from an emotional and socially awkward kid to achieving some level of success is not a new or shocking story. But these are the stories that inspire us, right? They are the stories we tend to connect to, because if you've ever felt broken like me, I understand. I get it. I do. So, yeah, apparently I'm a best-selling author. What do you care? What do I care, for that matter? I have no idea. There is so much to the story—so many of our stories never get told. Heck, I have a hard time even remembering some of them.

So, what's the point? You've picked up this book, and you're reading a chapter about boogers. Shouldn't I be over this already? Why do I feel so broken? I think there are things that are hard to let go of—things from the past that get stuck in the dark shadows of our emotional soul because they might be too painful, embarrassing, or just plain weird to bring up or dig out. When I find myself looming or lost in those shadows, on the days when I can't remember what it was like to be in the light, yeah, I feel pretty broken.

Broken like Me: An Insider's Toolkit for Mending Broken People is a book I wrote in an attempt to cast a brave light into those shadowy corners of my soul.* It's an insider's story, with parts of my story and the lessons I've learned and habits I've fostered because I'm tired and frustrated with the shadowy world. I want to obliterate the shadows.

In *I Understand: Pain, Love, and Healing after Suicide*, written by Vonnie Woodrick, who graciously invited me to participate in this book, Vonnie uses her story to let you know that you and your struggle can be understood and can shed a light on the misinformed perspectives of those who don't know what it's like to be in the shadows.† Vonnie shares her struggle toward strength and supportive community through her story. She and I have this in common: we believe every struggle is an opportunity.

Vonnie and I didn't write our books so that people would like us or think we're cool. This is another part of our story, one that, in part, is helping us survive. It's how we are living out hope day by day. The more stories that are out there, the more likely that people who feel broken, just like I do, will get help, build community, and create stability. This, in turn, will bless and have an impact on those who either can't or shouldn't share their story yet and those who haven't even begun to realize that their story even matters.

I've outlived the name "Joe-Booger," at least until my kids get ahold of this chapter. Vonnie has dealt with her great losses. We are moving forward. We haven't forgotten the past. The pain of our struggles and losses still haunts us from time to time. But we hope to do something more with them. I've learned to be patient, to live life like it's a marathon. Sure, I can tell you all day long that you're not alone. But with my story, my lived experience, I hope you are able to actually see and feel that you are not alone. And when you think that there is no point to your painful story, I hope you remember

---

* Joseph Reid, *Broken like Me: An Insider's Toolkit for Mending Broken People* (n.p.: Broken People, 2021).

† Vonnie Woodrick, *I Understand: Pain, Love, and Healing after Suicide* (Grand Rapids: Eerdmans, 2020).

that there are others who have painful stories, who feel all alone, who need to know that there is someone out there who knows their pain and who is finding their way out of the shadows too. Your story matters. Your experience and agony are not in vain. Find a "platform" when you've built a community of support, and when you're ready, share you story with anyone who will listen.

THE POWER OF LOVE

Living with Suicidal Thoughts

Bob Wilkie

I was alone, and I was scared. For the first time I put a plan together of how I could end the pain. In the Renaissance hotel in downtown Detroit, I stood in the window of my room looking out at the river thinking, *It's simple—go into the bathroom, slip the noose around your neck, and it will all go away.* I was twenty-four years old. I was playing in the NHL. To everyone around me I was living the dream, but for me, every day was a nightmare.

I remember asking myself, *How the hell did you end up here? What did you do to deserve this?* Unfortunately, there were no answers to the questions.

I made it through that night, more scared than ever because I had a plan. I had never before had a plan, only these awful thoughts. I continued to hide from those around me. I continued the struggle of living with the pain. I drank, I did drugs, because they were the only things that brought any kind of relief. I was disappointing those around me, my performance was inconsistent, and every day the weight became heavier. I'd think, *How much longer can I continue this?*

Then something amazing happened. I felt something I had not felt in a long time. Someone came into my life who didn't seem to care about who I was, or what I did. She showed affection and interest that was genuine. She did not want to do what everyone else did. This person saw the real me.

This was both terrifying and exhilarating at the same time: *If she ever finds out how I really feel, I am sure she would run away, or judge, or turn her back as others have. What do I do? Can I show her the real me? Can I share what I am thinking and feeling? Can I live without this again?* Still no answers came to me.

The days passed, and I did my best to hide my true self, but I had a real battle going on inside. One side was saying to trust, to let the love in, to show her. The other side was telling me that I would lose her, that she would be just like the rest, that I was setting myself up for more pain and suffering.

As a professional athlete, I had learned about resilience, about how to persevere, and I know that is what kept me alive. This was so different, though. This wasn't about some silly game; it was about me as a person. My heart felt whole again, I could feel things I had forgotten about, I could see things I had lost sight of, and I kept telling myself to keep pushing, so I did.

Like the booze and the drugs, it became addicting. I could not wait to hear her voice, to see her, to hold her, to hear her laugh, and to see the way she looked at me. It was love. I had not loved in so long. I had lost all the love in my life; it had turned to darkness and despair. This light was invigorating, and I wanted more of it. The thought of being without the love was no longer an option. I had to stand and fight for what I wanted, so I surged ahead.

Within a very short time (six months) we were married, and I felt safe. I felt valued. I could laugh again, smile again. I could breathe. We traveled together, taking on new adventures. We cooked and danced and sang. We shared our feelings and talked into the night. It was love—love had created this. I had opened myself up to it, I had embraced it, and it felt wonderful.

Years later we had a child. This was the most powerful experience of love that I had ever felt. I held her in my arms, trembling. She was so small, so helpless, just staring at me with beautiful blue eyes, and now I felt I had found my purpose: to be the best version of myself so that I could help her. I had to learn what had happened to me so I could fix it. If I was going to give this life a chance, I had to be better.

It was love. Love is a thing that makes life so special for humans. The loss of love is one of the most painful experiences we have; when our hearts are broken it can take away everything good that we had in our lives. We don't know when it will happen, or if it can happen, but when it does, we can become very jaded and think we cannot go through that again. So, we live our lives settling for less. We keep the walls up, the emotions locked away. We become skeptical and bitter. But we do not have to do that.

In the dictionary the definition of *love* is this: a profoundly tender, passionate affection for another person. That is what saved me. I felt this from another, really felt it, and was able to give it back. I was able to open my heart again, which I had once closed to avoid the pain.

Love grows; it is contagious and must be respected and fostered. Love is a work in progress, a commitment, a choice. We can lose it, but we cannot lose the desire to have it again. Love can save you. It can support you; it can change you. When we share love with another, we have power, a power much greater than we fully understand. Love ebbs and flows but should always be in our sights.

When we love, we can accomplish the greatest of things. When we can show it and share it, we can become an inspiration to others. To love we must learn how to love, how to accept it and be open to it. We must know that it could leave, and that is okay; we can love again.

I had lost my way, but it was love that helped me find it again. I have since lost the love of a career, a relationship, a parent, a child. But I have survived. Love is what keeps me going. I have learned to open myself up to all the love that the world has to offer. I search it out and create it whenever I get the chance. I now understand the power of love and all that it requires.

Today I work to help people. I help them learn and understand things about themselves. I help them see what they have created in their lives and help guide them to the life they want, to the solution that eases the pain. I help them to find love again in order to live the life they want so desperately. I have seen miraculous things happen when people find love and let it in to their lives again. It makes them look younger, it helps them make better decisions, it helps them move out of the darkness and into the light, and it is all because they decided to kick down the walls and give it another go.

Some would think this to be hokey—I get it. I was once there too. I implore you, if you are feeling any of the things I have described here, to begin the search for love. On my journey an exercise I had to do was to stand in front of a mirror and tell myself, "I love you." It took more than six months for me to believe this. It is an exercise I still do today almost fifteen years later. I remind myself constantly because to have something so powerful you must practice daily to be capable of holding it.

Love is what gave me my family, love is what gives me purpose, love is what helps me through the tough times, and love is what helps me keep things in the proper perspective. In a world full of hate, love is what can heal us. Hate destroys good things. Love creates them. The world today is a difficult and sometimes ominous place. The news spreads hate and fear; the politicians do the same. The challenge to spread, share, and find love has never been greater. But I can tell you from my personal experiences that we must *let love rule*. If you *let love rule* your life, it will be a life you will be proud to have lived. What you can do for others is desperately needed. Tear down the walls, fight through the pain and chaos, to find it. It will provide you with all that you need.

We only need one true ruler, and that is love. Love what you do and whom you do it with; love the imperfections; love yourself so that you can love others. Love will help you forgive, it will help you learn patience, and it will create understanding and compassion.

If we all loved a little bit more, what impact would it have on the world?

FINDING EMPOWERMENT

Living with Suicidal Ideation

Maddie Woodrick

I have always been proud of my candidness when it comes to talking about uncomfortable topics. Suicide, suicide prevention, and experiences related to mental health are a few that come up quite a bit. Maybe it's because I've worked in an addiction and mental-health treatment center since graduating from college; maybe it's because my mom founded and runs a nonprofit organization whose purpose is to erase the stigma associated with mental health and suicide; maybe it's because four generations within my family have met their untimely death at the hands of one of the most unforgiving illnesses: depression.

I'm proud of my candidness because I have been desensitized to the weight those terms carry for many people. I have been able to converse about this topic, not because I felt as if it affected me personally, but because of the many people in my life who did. I believed that by speaking on their behalf and not mine, I was able to understand the complexities of my own mental health. That is true in a lot of ways, but I have always skipped over a lot.

Writing has always been something that I believed came easy to me. In fourth grade, I was reassured by a teacher that writing is something that I was good at and needed to continue to pursue. This meant a lot because, throughout my life, I didn't think I was especially good at anything. When it came to school, sports, and hobbies, I was painfully average and sometimes below average—except when it came to writing. Language arts was the first class I was excited to challenge myself in, and I wanted to continue challenging myself. So, I chose that as my degree in college: English writing. Academically and socially, I had my hurdles, hurdles that at times seemed impossible to get over. For instance, my sophomore year of college was the first time a professor or teacher had ever told me, "I don't think writing is for you." At the time, I brushed this off and said to myself, "I don't care what he says; I know I'm good." Externally, I began making changes to completely alter what I wanted my outcome of attending college to be. I no longer wanted to be a writer; I wanted to be a lawyer, or something that I felt was more attainable than being a writer.

I was able to finish my degree with English writing, but I added a double minor in social justice and legal studies to ensure a more realistic career path. I was excited to attend my senior seminar class for my degree because our final project was a piece of writing that could be written in any format about anything that I wanted. At the time, my mom was also in the process of writing her book: *I Understand: Pain, Love, and Healing after Suicide.*

However, as soon as I began the writing process for this project, I felt defeated.

The premise of my senior seminar project was essentially a memoir of my life. I don't think my life story is especially exciting or more traumatic than that of the person next to me, but I do believe that I can articulate my experiences in a way that would hopefully connect with people. Through sharing my experiences and my families' experiences with mental health, suicide, pain, and loss, I hoped that someone might read it and say, "I know what you're talking about." I had a similar revelation after I read Mariel Hemingway's book, which inspired me to begin writing blogs in the first place. Although writing this book and sharing my story was what I believed I was meant to do, I felt defeated because I underestimated the emotional toll that writing this would have on me.

I don't really remember my childhood, because depression is linked to memory loss. So, when I began writing chapters about specific family interactions, I relied heavily on my mom and my sister to help me fill in the gaps. I was shocked at some of the situations that I didn't remember, and a lot of the time, I felt extremely heartbroken about the reality.

I was able to muster up enough emotional capacity to finish my school assignment, but after that I refused to continue writing or even look at what I had written. Simply put, it was too painful. I'm proud of what I wrote; that's not the issue. When it came to memories associated with my father, I enjoyed hearing about my time with him, but I also got really sad thinking that a lot of the experiences I shared in my writing assignment wouldn't have happened if he was still alive. I felt that, if he was alive, he could have saved me from a lot of the emotional turmoil that continued to happen throughout the rest of my life.

In my assignment I also wrote about my experience going to a new school my freshman year of high school and moving in with my mom's fiancé and his family. My intention in writing was to be honest about everything, but I didn't include the bullying that took place at that new school and the intense feelings of suicidal ideation I experienced when I was fourteen. I think the tipping point for me when I felt as if I could never write my own book was realizing that I would have to put my entire being out there and that everyone in my life would perceive me in a much different light than the one I had created.

All those memories and feelings that I spent years trying to bury and forget about, all those memories and feelings that I associate with immense shame, were brought up again.

My blogs and what I thought I was good at when it came to my writing were centered on my own experiences with mental health and suicide. After I realized I wouldn't be writing my own book anytime soon, I deemed myself a failure. I believed that I wasn't emotionally strong enough to write this book right now, but deep down I didn't think I would ever be.

When my school year finished and the feelings I felt after turning in my senior seminar assignment were so fresh, I began feeling extremely depressed, and feelings of suicide ideation crept into my head again. This period, just like when I was fourteen, was when I genuinely felt as if there was no light at the end of the tunnel for me. I have always experienced depression, but when my mom or therapist asked me if I was suicidal, I genuinely told them no because I was excited for my future. Within these two time periods, however, the excitement was extinguished. It wasn't that I hated my life; I genuinely didn't think I was adequate for the life I had or the life I thought I always wanted.

Luckily, I was able to work through some of those feelings, and honestly, I still am. I believe that telling someone how you are feeling is one of the most important steps when it comes to dealing with mental health issues. The times I felt at my strongest emotionally were when I felt connected with other people or was actively having conversations about my mental health. I was able to talk to my mom about these feelings; I hate asking for help, but I knew I needed it, and I knew I needed someone to know in case something happened.

I began the process of trying to find a medication that could help me; and I say "process" because it really is one. When it comes to anxiety and depression, there isn't a cure that works for everyone. Some medications that work great for other people made me either feel worse or feel nothing at all; unfortunately, it's trial and error. Although I had been in therapy while I attended college in Illinois, I realized it was important for me to find a therapist while I was home in Michigan. To this day, I am so happy I made those decisions for myself. Once I found a medication that worked and a therapist that I looked forward to talking to every week, my emotional health went up exponentially. I'm not "fixed"—I'm still depressed and anxious—but on the days I make decisions that are good for me, I know that I'm adding another day to my life, and I'm really excited about what this life has to offer me. Maybe I'll write a book, maybe I won't; that's not the point. I need to accept all the good and the bad that has happened to me and work to use the bad to empower me, instead of using it as a weapon against me to fuel those feelings of inadequacy.

SPEAKING THE UNSPEAKABLE

Living with Suicidal Thoughts

Scott Teichmer

Just what is my story? I am a suicide-attempt survivor; I have also survived countless thoughts of suicide, which at periods throughout my life were ceaseless and unrelenting. You won't often hear stories like mine, but many such stories exist in nearly every community across nearly every demographic.

Our societal inclination, however, has been to talk about suicide only after a person has died by suicide (that is, if we even talk about it at all). Nonsuicide, on the other hand, has largely remained a nonstory. This needs to change.

We have all read far too many beautiful tributes to those who have died by suicide, memorials to those overcome by hopelessness and pain, some having struggled with suicidal thoughts for years, some even for decades. We read their stories, we grieve for their families, we might even quietly grieve our own losses, and then the subject of suicide fades back to silence until the next tragedy occurs.

When I read these stories, I can all too easily put myself in the shoes of the deceased. There can be a comfort, and dare I even say, allure, in imagining such an outpouring of love and compassion from beyond the grave. While many tributes and memorials can be beautiful, I can't help but think how much more beautiful, how much more meaningful, those tributes would be if we could make them while those individuals were still alive, still surviving and persisting, still resisting and overcoming those thoughts of ultimate escape, and most importantly, still living, breathing, and walking among us on this earth.

I recently read the story of a young man who had died by suicide. His family described him as someone who had often looked out for others, even to a fault. They described his long-standing struggles with depression and anxiety, and they shared a remarkable story from the previous year, when he had gotten a semicolon tattoo, a symbol of hope. It was the word *warr;or* with a semicolon boldly taking the place of the letter *i*, thoughtfully inscribed by a family member who is a tattoo artist.

Now that would have been one heck of a story, but we missed it. The public outpouring of love and compassion should have come around that event of getting the tattoo, not his death, and should have been in celebration of this young man's courage, his strength, his honesty, and his vulnerability. This should have been a story of survival, of overcoming, and of his family's loving support, so how did we miss it? How could this have been yet another nonstory, the details of which were only to be revealed after his death? This needs to change.

Much like this young man, I, too, had long-standing struggles with anxiety and depression. After trying a laundry list of different medications and regimens throughout the years, I was eventually given the label of "treatment-resistant depression." The pain, the hopelessness, the detachment from self, and the increasing disconnection from life all brought me to the point of attempting suicide. I felt I had no other choice.

I had actually set off with the intent to end my life on a number of prior occasions but was thankfully always able to stop myself. This time was different. This time I told myself I had to go through with it no matter what. I believe there was still a small part of me that didn't want to die, that was hanging on by the tiniest whisper of a thread, but the shameful parts of me spoke at an overwhelming decibel of such severity and harshness. They told me that I didn't belong on this earth, that I was forever a failure and a bad person, and that I didn't deserve to be alive.

I can now see this relentless barrage of shameful thoughts for the lies that they are: mere distortions, misperceptions, and miscalculations, but at the time, they were my reality. The neural networks of our brains are shaped through experience; and as we develop our early concepts in infancy, we continue to refine and create new concepts throughout our life span, but sometimes things go awry. The unique ability to combine and create increasingly abstract concepts is a huge part of what makes humanity just so remarkably adaptable to a wide variety of environments. Because of this, we can potentially come up with an infinite number of solutions to any given problem, but this conceptual ability also has its costs. It can lead us to solutions that might not be useful, even to some that might ultimately be maladaptive, such as the concept of suicide.

In many ways, one could describe mental illness as occurring when our brain's predictions, including those of our sensory experiences, emotional concepts, and thoughts, do not match objective reality. For many, correcting these patterns of prediction error and faulty concepts will be a lengthy, work-intensive process requiring the help of mental-health professionals. While this is true, I believe that the most crucial component for making a shift toward healing and recovery is that of human connection and understanding.

Following my suicide attempt and release from the hospital, one of the first things I did was look for a support group for attempt survivors. I was in search of connection and understanding, as my attempt had left me feeling increasingly ashamed and alone. Unfortunately, I quickly realized that supports specific to suicide-attempt survivors were practically nonexistent, as my search only turned up loss-survivor support groups. Even my mental-health treatment, which included both psychiatric and counseling services, tended to regard suicidal thoughts and behaviors merely as side effects and did not target them directly with suicide-specific interventions. I was left to deal with my thoughts of suicide, and now my suicide attempt, alone in shame, in isolation, and in secrecy.

It wasn't until I got my bachelor's degree in psychology and began working in behavioral health that I really began to heal. The skills that I was learning to teach and help others also became the skills that I would use to heal myself. Eventually, I got a job at my county's community mental-health agency and joined the suicide-prevention coalition. While I still experienced occasional thoughts of suicide, they were becoming more manageable, and I was now better able to cope with life's stressors. My suicide attempt and my struggles with suicidal thoughts, however, remained a shameful secret.

I believe that in many ways shame leads to silence, and silence leads to more shame, but we can break this cycle. Through my involvement with the suicide-prevention coalition, I eventually got to the point where I was able publicly to share my story with others. By sharing lived experience, we have the potential to alleviate the stigma and shame that can so often surround experiences of suicide, including thoughts, attempts, and loss. At coalition meetings and at suicide-prevention trainings and events, I began habitually introducing myself as a suicide-attempt survivor. In doing so, my intention was not only to share my personal connection to suicide but also to help break the stigma, the silence, and the shame.

I also became a QPR (Question, Persuade, Refer) gatekeeper instructor and master trainer through the QPR Institute. Just as CPR teaches lifesaving skills for a cardiac crisis, QPR teaches lifesaving skills for a suicide crisis, and it is the most widely taught suicide-prevention gatekeeper training in the world. I would use my own personal story to deliver some of the key training concepts. Sharing my lived experience has helped make these trainings especially impactful and has also provided me with the rewarding sense of creating purpose out of my pain.

Throughout the following years, I had the opportunity to attend multiple suicide-prevention conferences, where I was able to witness other suicide-attempt survivors sharing their lived experiences with immense courage and vulnerability. I finally had a glimpse of that peer-to-peer connection and understanding that I had sought following my suicide attempt so many years ago. This harking back led to inspiration: if a support group for suicide-attempt survivors did not exist, I would create one.

Our Suicide-Attempt Survivors Support Group was formed and was the first peer support group of its kind in the state of Michigan. In the beginning, the group's other original cofacilitator and I both wondered, "Would anyone actually show up?" Studies suggest that there are approximately thirty suicide attempts for every one death by suicide, so we could infer that there might be upward of one thousand suicide attempts in our county each year. That's a lot of people, but we also knew that stigma, shame, and a variety of other barriers might make it a difficult group to show up to for the first time. We were both resolute, however, and agreed that even if no one came, we would continue to offer the group, with the thought that just having such a group publicly available might make headway against the prevailing and pervasive stigma.

What started as a local support group has now grown to include members from across the nation, after transitioning to a virtual format. Because there are so few support groups of its kind in the United States and even globally, the increasingly widespread interest, as well as our growing size, unfortunately led us to create a waitlist for out-of-state participants. I felt great internal struggle with turning people away, knowing firsthand the pain, the loneliness, and the hopelessness that can accompany suicidal thoughts and suicide attempt. I also knew the immense hope that such group would have provided me following my attempt those years ago. I contemplated, *There must be something else I can do to help people feel less alone, to feel understood, and to feel validated and affirmed in a way similar to peer support.* I again reflected on my own experiences of how secrecy, silence, and shame had become life-threatening and nearly fatal; and the idea of *Speak the Unspeakable* arose.

This brings my story up to the present day. In what has seemed like a whirlwind of a few months, I have been able to develop and launch *Speak the Unspeakable*, a video series focused on suicide prevention through the lens of lived experience. By using my firsthand knowledge with suicidal thoughts and behaviors to educate, engage, and empower viewers, I am allowing my lived experience not only to serve as a primary source of valuable information and insight but, more importantly, to break down the stigma and shame often surrounding experiences of suicide.

Recent studies have shown that, for individuals who have had suicidal ideation or made a suicide attempt in the past year, reading a personal account from someone who has already overcome a similar crisis can have a strong preventive effect. So, when addressing the subject of suicide, if we omit lived experience from the discussion, we are omitting important stories of coping and of survival, and we are omitting valuable sources of wisdom and hope. Our stories need to be told.

THE BATTLE WITHIN

Living with an Eating Disorder

Sarah Fialk

Struggling with an eating disorder is never easy, and the holidays can be especially difficult as the media's focus on weight loss is at an all-time high. However, don't let that fool you into thinking that eating disorders are all about the food and body. The real issue for most of us who have struggled is control—or as I like to say it, my eating disorder was a way to manage a world that often feels unmanageable.

What does that mean? When I was highly anxious or my world felt like it was chaotic or in others' hands more than my own (for example, grades, others' opinions of me, and career choices), creating rules around food and exercise gave me a sense of security. I am a perfectionist, which means I like everything to feel "clean" or "organized," and I want to be my best in every way I can—in school, at work, in relationships, and, yes, in my physical appearance. Following certain diets or lifestyles (such as cleanses, shakes, or veganism) often looks like a noble pursuit of health, but sometimes it's a way to create and follow rules to the letter in at least one area of life. If I ever dared to veer away from those rules, however, my inner critic made me pay for it. At my core, all I wanted was to find predictability in a world that often felt anything but.

An interesting—and sad—result of living with an eating disorder is how much it restricts not only our food intake but our lives as a whole. Sure, I may have appeared on the outside to have control over food and exercise and over every other piece of my life, but with the physical, mental, and emotional effects of the life I was leading (such as weakness, fixation on food, dizziness, anxiety), I couldn't be fully available for friends, extracurriculars, or family. Ironically, trying to maintain control completely took away what control I had in the first place. In the moment, it felt worth it. I felt if I didn't restrict my intake or exercise exactly according to my routine, I would panic even more, so it wasn't an option to give it up. Life felt unbearable, but I didn't at all believe it would get better if I took away my very effective coping mechanism! I, the one who seemed fine on the outside, couldn't understand why anyone around me believed that life was enjoyable.

I know now that eating a variety of foods and moving in a way that brings me joy gives me balance and freedom. My recovery continues to be a work in progress, but I can more easily eat with friends now, without adhering to strict rules and without fearing others' judgment of what's on my plate.

I have a much better understanding that "health" is physical, mental, *and* emotional, so even if the food in front of me doesn't fit society's idea of nutritional, my mind and body are much stronger when I can be flexible and live in the moment when at a restaurant with a friend who wants to order dessert. I no longer plan ahead what I'll eat or when I'll exercise; there are no rules to follow. I am still working on finding effective coping skills to help me tolerate my sensitivity, anxiety, loneliness, and often-high emotions, and I am exploring my relationship with exercise so that it becomes fun and not compulsive. So, no, every day is not a cake walk. (Sorry, had to!) Some days it feels as if I have a long way to go, but today I don't look at food as a way to cope with internal or external chaos. Facing overwhelming thoughts and feelings head on, as opposed to using unhealthy skills, requires a lot of bravery, and because of that, for the first time in a long time, I can say that I feel proud of myself.

TELLING THE TRUTH

Living with Addiction

Kathy Slagter

I released a bloodcurdling scream, then another and another. Why? I had caused pain to my children because of my addiction. The last thing a mother wants to do is hurt her children, and yet I put them in harm's way, for years, because I chose alcohol over them time and time again. I was filled with deep regret. I needed to let it go. I was with a coach, an audience of supportive women, and a horse. I now know resentments, even toward oneself, are the number-one reason people go back to drinking, and since staying sober means life or death for me, I screamed.

As a young girl in ninth grade, fifteen years old, I had my first beer, and as the saying goes, one is too many, and one thousand is not enough. It was game on from that point forward. My group of friends and I were at a drive-in theater, beers in the trunk, all excited to experience drinking. I took my first sip, and too quickly the last beer was gone, and I wanted more—I always wanted more.

I was a shy girl, quiet in nature, yet wanting so desperately to be outgoing and comfortable in crowds. I had a great group of friends to hang out with, I was a cheerleader, and I played a few sports. From the outside looking in it may have seemed as though I had it all together, yet on the inside I felt alone, lost, and uncomfortable.

I quickly figured out that if I drank a few beers, I could change my personality. I became outgoing, chatty, and more confident. Without a drink in my hand, I stood on the outside of my group of friends, but hand me a beer, and that liquid courage gave me the strength to step into the crowd. So I found that the more I drank, the easier it was to hide my shyness. My problem was I never knew when to stop. I would shift myself from shy to outgoing to stupid drunk. I then became another version of myself I didn't like.

I wanted to find a happy medium and stay there, but that was not possible for this drinking gal. I knew that I drank differently from others. I would drink twice as many beers, or if we bought a bottle, I would always drink more than my equal share. That's when I started hiding my drinking. I would buy my own bottle, or have a few before I met up with friends. I never wanted to appear drunk, but I loved to drink.

Drinking became my "best friend"—one that got me into a lot of trouble, but also encouraged me to do many things outside of my comfort zone. If you imagine grabbing the hand of your best friend for courage, that was me with my alcohol. Unfortunately, my bestie also led me down a dangerous road, one that could very well have killed me.

All of my major life happenings—making girlfriends, dating boyfriends, getting engaged, marrying, and getting pregnant—revolved around drinking. At the time, I would say I was having fun, and I can say I did enjoy my life growing up, yet today, I know I missed the meaning behind all the events. My thinking was all centered around alcohol. I would show up in the flesh, yet I wasn't present. I lived my life with a good buzz on.

A pivotal moment in my life was learning I was pregnant. I was thrilled. I was also conflicted because I knew this meant I would have to go nine months without a drink. I also made the decision to bottle-feed instead of breastfeed my child because I wanted my bottle of beer. This went on for all three of my children. I did not drink during all of my pregnancies. The health of my children was more important to me than drinking. I clinged on to the fact that I could stop drinking if I needed to, so to me that meant that I wasn't an alcoholic.

In my twenties, most of my drinking was on the weekends, and by my thirties I would have a girls' night out, during the weekdays, to get away and be Kathy, not mommy. I was a stay-at-home mom and I had a small daycare in my home, so having "me time" was rare. When I did have the opportunity to go out, I always had too many—I would get wasted. As a mother of young children, I put them in danger. I'm sure I passed out, or had black-out moments. If my children were to need me, I would not have heard them cry or have been able to properly handle an emergency.

As the years went by my children began to notice mommy's drinking. I remember the first time my drinking became an embarrassment to them; at least it was the first time I was aware that my drunkenness caused them to be ashamed of me. At this time, we lived about four hours away from our parents, so coming home was a vacation of sorts. It was Christmas Eve and celebration began early for me, with morning mimosas (orange juice and champagne) and later Bloody Marys (vodka and tomato juice), then in the afternoon I broke open a bottle of rum and continued to drink way too many rum and Cokes.

My husband and children were with me, and we arrived at my mother's home around four in the afternoon for a Christmas Eve party with a group of around thirty friends and family. And I was already very drunk. I could hardly walk, was slurring my words, and was loud and obnoxious. And of course, I thought I was the life of the party. The next morning, with an insane hangover, I had to look my crying children in the eyes, as they told me how scared they were to see me so drunk. Yet, that didn't stop me from getting intoxicated again and again, scaring them many times over the decades of my drinking career.

My babies became teens, and since my life was centered around partying, I gave my children permission to follow in my footsteps. I allowed them to have friends over and have their own parties. I would look the other way, because I believed that to have fun, one must add alcohol. I drank as a child, so how could I ask my children not to drink? I turned out fine, right? I had a husband, a family, friends, a nice home, fun toys, and money in the bank. Slowly drinking was becoming a dangerous game jeopardizing not only my well-being but also that of my children.

Not only was being aware of the law and police and having my lawyer on speed dial a grim reality, but now my body was starting to show signs of alcoholism. As I turned fifty, I began every day with a cocktail, adding vodka to my orange juice. My body was screaming at me for more alcohol; I was shaking, quivering from the inside out. I was vomiting every morning, my urine was blood red, and I couldn't eat most days. The only remedy that helped was to add more alcohol. I even went to the hospital a few times because I thought I was having a heart attack. I was frightened that I was going to die, yet I was even more afraid of living without alcohol, so I continued to drink.

For three years, I lived addicted to alcohol, drinking 24-7, not because I wanted to but because I had to. I would hide a gallon bottle of vodka in my bedroom closet to fill the one in the kitchen when no one was looking. After a few hours without a drink, my body would start to let me know by shaking, so I would fill water bottles up with alcohol and had one with me at all times. Nights were the scariest times for me. On my bedside table was a glass of ice water, which of course was iced vodka. I would lie in bed and feel my heart racing. On the nights I didn't pass out, I prayed that I would make it to the morning. I knew my heart was working overtime to keep me alive, yet the first thing I would do in the morning was pour myself another drink, because I was afraid to face my reality. I needed help, I was a drunk, and I was dying.

I would have a few moments of clarity and would attempt to get sober, but time and time again I would eventually end up drunk. I fortunately had a bad case of poison ivy, making it necessary for me to make an appointment to see my doctor. During my checkup, she noticed my blood pressure was dangerously high and was extremely concerned. She asked me to come back the next week to recheck.

I canceled—I knew my drinking was the reason and I wasn't ready to admit out loud, even to my doctor, that I had a problem.

That was July, and in September of 2011, I finally reached out to my best friend, human this time, to be with me as I told my husband I was ready to get help. Admitting my alcoholism to him and then to my children, who were ranging then from seventeen to twenty-one years old, was heart-wrenching both for me and for them. I knew I had to be brave, yet I was scared. I felt worthless and filled with shame and disgust, about as low as one could feel about themselves. I guess this is a good description of reaching my bottom.

I went to a rehabilitation center for seven days. It took three days to cure the shakes, and during my stay I saw the therapist one time, and I went to mandatory group meetings and Alcoholics Anonymous (AA) meetings every day. Upon release, my blood pressure and heart rate were normal, and I was feeling so much better. They prescribed me an anxiety medication to help with my anxiousness that developed without the calming effect of alcohol.

When I returned home, I went to bars, joined my friends at happy hour, and did not continue going to AA. I was not willing to do anything but prove I was strong enough to be around alcohol and not drink. I was sober for twenty-one days.

I remember that first drink, the burn of the alcohol going down my throat; it felt like a big hug from a long-lost best friend. And yet again, my friend quickly became my archenemy. I reverted to hiding, lying, and pretending I was sober for four more months. I was building a wall of shame and hatred for who I had become. I played the game of not drinking for a week, and then drinking for two weeks, sobering up, and getting drunk, over and over. Maybe I had to prove to myself, again, that I could not control my drinking, because eventually I would get drunk.

I went back to a rehabilitation center for thirty days, and I found I had to stir up my bravery from within. For most of my lifetime I used alcohol as a way to gain courage. Now I know I must face life without alcohol. I now have to do it alone. I lost my alcoholic courage. I had to reach deep inside myself to find my strength. I had to be brave enough, to do it afraid.

My old insecurities I had as a teen started to arise. I reverted to being my quiet self, and my self-confidence was lost. In a crowd or all by myself, I felt alone. I didn't feel as though I fit in or belonged anywhere.

I wondered who I was as a mother, wife, daughter, sister. Every relationship changed when I became sober. Slowly I began to find my way, one day at a time. My therapist asked me to find a hobby I was passionate about, and I knew right away it was horses. I started volunteering at a special-needs riding stable. I loved being around horses and seeing the children relax and ride with so much joy.

I owned a quarter horse for years before becoming sober, yet I rarely rode her. I moved her to a local barn, one that had an indoor arena, and I started to get myself comfortable in the saddle again. This barn had a program for young girls to heal in the presence of horses, not a riding program. This opened a path for me that I am still on—working with those in recovery, copartnering with horses.

After some searching, I found Touched by a Horse, and I became an Equine Gestalt Master Coach. This intensive two-year program taught me not only to nurture my love for horses and the magic they can bring to our lives but also to look deep within myself and to clear away the shame and hatred I had for my old way of living.

When the fog was lifted and my past became very clear to me, I had sadness and grief for all I missed and allowed to happen while I was drinking. One of my greatest regrets and deepest sorrows is who I was as a mother to my beautiful children: choosing to drink, staying out late, drinking and driving, not understanding the fear this brought to my children. I feel embarrassment and disappointment about how I conducted myself, slurring words, drinking around them and their friends.

My recovery date is February 11, 2012. My youngest child was eighteen when I finally became sober. That's a lot of built-up years of resentment. I needed a safe place to work through my past mistakes. And Melisa Pearce, the founder of Touched by a Horse, gave me the opportunity with her healing horses' hearts open wide to support and guide me through the process of letting the pain go, so I might step into a new and loving relationship with my children.

She held space for me to talk openly about who I was as a mother and about some of my mistakes that haunted me. She allowed me to get to my pain, feel into the deep ache inside, until all that was left was a scream—a full-belly, let-it-go release. I screamed and cried and bellowed my anger until it was all released into the universe, on her sandy arena floor. With her beloved horses supporting me, my teacher and fellow peers who, like me, were also becoming coaches held me in their arms and gave me the love I needed to receive to heal.

Because of that day in the barn, I can wear my mistakes like a loose garment. My relationship with each of my children continues to grow. I have had some very deep conversations with them about their journey with me, have made apologies and have been forgiven, but as life goes, we always have more work to do.

I am now a coach who copartners with my horses, helping others find their passion and purpose in their lives. I hold space for others to release their screams, I listen to their cries, and I allow them to experience my healing horses' powerful energy, which horses so freely give to us humans. Today, I am grateful and thankful to be free from the bondage of alcoholism. Staying sober has to be a priority in my life, so I can continue to stay present and available for my God, children, and grandchildren. As my horses and I coach each other in recovery, I now give it away so I can keep it.

NEVER TOO LATE

Living with Alcohol

Steve Kelly

As someone who regularly relays health stories and statistics and who facilitates very personal conversations about things like addiction, mental illness, and suicide, I think I've become pretty accustomed to it. I've been in radio for over forty years, twelve at WOOD radio, my dream job. I must admit, however, that although I've shared countless personal experiences, such as calling the station right after our babies were born and sharing our challenges with being empty nesters, I've purposely left much out of the conversation.

After reading yet another story about addiction and suicide on the rise in America, I reached out to Vonnie to join us in studio. During the interview, Vonnie's bravery, honesty, and vulnerability helped unlock my heart. The Sunday after that interview was Father's Day. My youngest, Maddie, who is friends with Vonnie's Maddie, wrote in her card to me, "Continue to use your voice to impact the lives of many." My Maddie has volunteered with i understand and even attempted to bring a chapter to Xavier University, where she studies marketing. I don't believe in coincidences.

After prayer and reflection, a few days later I spoke to a local Rotary club and bridged the topic for the first time publicly by saying, "Maybe one of you is struggling now. Perhaps you're on a slippery slope. It may help you to know that I'm an alcoholic in recovery. I've been to the meetings in church basements; I've been through extensive therapy. With the help of my God, my family, and some physical- and mental-health professionals, I have been sober for over five and a half years. However dark it may seem, I promise you that it's not too late. But it must start with you. Lay it on the altar, talk to a cherished friend, even your physician. There is help and there is hope, and you are not alone." My words came naturally, and they were very well received. Since my initial presentation I've told my story to whoever asks, thanks to i understand.

My father was also an alcoholic, but his story doesn't end on a high note. He lost his battle with depression and dependency, and he ended his life. He was fifty-two. He never met my beautiful wife or our amazing daughters. He was brilliant. I have been angry, I have disrespected his memory because of my ignorance, and I have been ashamed to speak openly about it, especially after my own battles with the disease—that is, until my encounter with the lifesaving non-profit group i understand.

Every day I pray to be of service, so I know that's why I'm sharing my story. I pray that by sharing these things, which I've been able to edit out of my public persona, to whoever will hear, that it will help them. Look at the people God has put in your life. Look for the signs or coincidences that point *you* toward help. Most importantly, in the words of R.E.M.'s "Everybody Hurts," "Hold on, everybody hurts sometimes!"

I'm Steve Kelly, proud husband to Sandy, father to Caitlin and Madison. I survived a nervous or mental breakdown, I have been treated for clinical depression with generalized anxiety, I'm an alcoholic, and now I understand.

two
Stories of Love

THE LOVE BETWEEN A MOTHER AND DAUGHTER

Losing a Child

Julie Gregory

My beautiful daughter was born on April 17, 1986, and died on March 10, 2015. Her death certificate says she died by a gunshot wound. That's only part of the truth. That doesn't explain the real cause, which is mental illness, more specifically depression and bipolar disorder.

Jessica was in the top twenty of her high school class of 2004. She was in sideline cheer as well as the competitive cheer team, she ran track, and she had three amazing friends. She also had a little brother, Clayton, who was fourteen years younger than her, but they were great friends.

She was far from perfect; I know she smoked, and I know she tried some drugs and drinking, but she kept up her grades and was very responsible. After high school she attended Aquinas College and graduated in 2008. Soon after she was working at a local behavioral-health treatment center as an administrative secretary. She was also a personal assistant to one of the doctors for a year. She loved that so much.

People would come and go in that office, and at some point, her supervisor and office manager were new. These two supervisors did not display professional behavior to Jes; they liked to push her buttons. Jes was a perfectionist; everything needed to be done exactly right, and she would really take it to heart if she was told that things were not right. She tried and tried to be and do everything they expected from her. The younger of the two was always threatening

Jessica. They both knew she had some anxieties, and they played on them every chance they could. Basically, the office manager would say she would be written up or fired if something was done wrong. Lots of pressure was put on Jes, and the workload was getting to a point where she felt as if they were setting her up to fail. My daughter was being bullied.

On January 31, 2014, I received a call from the supervisor telling me I had to pick Jes up from work. She had experienced a breakdown at work and needed to go to the emergency room. So, I picked her up at work and drove her to the ER. This is where it got real for me. I learned my daughter's "happy thoughts" were of death. She had been self-harming, and she wanted to die. After a few tests at the hospital, they released her to me with the understanding that I take her directly to the local mental-health hospital. We drove there and checked in. I sat quietly and listened to all the questions and answers from the intake person and my daughter. This all got so real so fast.

She was admitted and stayed in the hospital for about two weeks. Her family and friends visited her every chance we could. She somehow managed to get special "visits" from me. I have no idea how, but they allowed her visits from me anytime she needed me. She was diagnosed with bipolar disorder, depression, anxiety issues, and thyroid issues. She went to outpatient therapy for a week and then continued seeing a counselor and psychiatrist until the day she died.

Then her workplace called her. Well, it was her two bosses I spoke of earlier, who asked for a meeting. On the day of the meeting, March 11, 2014, she was on FMLA or maybe short-term disability. She thought that she was going in to find out when she could go back to work. To her surprise, they fired her at that meeting, and they dated the firing back to January 31, when she had her breakdown. They also told all the staff at the clinic to break ties with Jes or risk losing their own jobs. This was the proverbial straw that broke the camel's back. She signed the papers she was asked to sign and walked out of the office. She went home and called me. By the time I arrived, she had cut herself. It wasn't deep; she wasn't trying to end her life.

I asked her why she had done this, and she told me it made her feel better inside.

We called the mental hospital and brought her back in, only this time she was unemployed, and she thought there was no insurance. Of course, the hospital needed to know they would get their money. We worked that all out, and she stayed just a few more days and was released. They taught her coping skills, and she was doing pretty well on all the medications she was on. During this time, she kept a journal. Of course, we didn't know this until later.

Trying to find a job after a breakdown was difficult. Doors were slammed in her face, and the growing feeling of not being good enough played a toll on her. Her savings account was dwindling, and she was stressed about losing her apartment. She spent months and months applying and interviewing. She spent almost every evening with me, her dad, and her brother. We knew things were hard, but we thought that if she was still seeing us every night, we could help her get through all of this. She even did a job shadow at a local hospital, a job that looked very promising. We think that she would have gotten that job because the person who interviewed her called just a day too late. He left a message on her cell phone on March 11, 2015, the day after she lost her battle.

On March 9, 2015, Jessica came to our house, and we all had dinner together. After dinner, Jes and I put a jigsaw puzzle together. We finished one and started a new puzzle that she picked out. I even made the comment, "Really? That's a hard one; it's going to take forever!" She explained that she liked that one; it was pretty. So, we started on this new puzzle. Little did I know about nine hours before this she had gone to a store and purchased a handgun. About 10:30 p.m. I got tired. We took care of the puzzle table, and she left. That was the last time I would see my daughter alive. She drove home and parked her car in her carport. She entered her apartment, hung up her coat, placed her laptop and phone on her bed with sticky notes on them with the passwords written down, and placed her journal on her bed.

She wrote me one last letter saying, "I'm sorry, Mom. I love you." There was more written, but for now this is all I can share. She shut her bedroom door, to keep her beloved cat Desiré out of the room, and she silently ended the pain she had been tortured with for exactly one year.

On March 10, 2015, I tried texting her all day, and when she didn't answer, I finally headed over to her apartment, where I found her in her bedroom, lying on the floor.

Her story isn't over. We will continue to say her name and tell her story. We will break down those walls of stigma about suicide and mental illness. We found a card in her car a few days later; it's her mission in her own handwriting: "My mission in life is to make a positive difference in others' lives. I want to help others become better people. I want them to look at me for inspiration and ask for my help, if they need or want it. I believe my purpose in this world is to make other people believe they too have a purpose." We will continue her mission for as long as we can.

LIFE AFTER DAD

Losing a Parent

Molly McNamara

I remember being at work when the phone rang for me. It was the fall of 1989, a Friday afternoon, when my dad called to see how I was doing. Was I happy? Was life good in Steamboat Springs? I reassured him that all was well, and I had successfully flown the nest! My dad used to say, "The greatest gift we can give our children is roots and wings." When I hung up the phone, I exclaimed to my boss, "My dad said I love you, first!" I had always said it first, and then he would say, "I love you too."

That weekend, I did not hear from my family back home. Life was good, and I was working and living in a ski town, all by myself. It was a big growing-up time for me, after finally leaving my family back home in Michigan. I was very attached to my hometown roots, but at twenty-four years old, my dad thought I should spread my wings! He suggested I leave Grand Rapids behind and try something new in Colorado. Later I realized he was pushing me forward, away from our town, to prepare me for his passing.

Monday morning the phone rang again for me, but this time it was my dear, sweet brother Johnny. The first thing he said to me was to sit down. He then told me our dad had died. I immediately thought it was a plane crash, as I knew he was heading to Pepperdine University to apply for a teaching position in trial law within the coming months. My brother said he had taken his life. I had no idea what he was saying! I barely knew what suicide was, let alone that my dad would have done such a thing. It was incomprehensible that my dad was gone and that he had taken his own life. In shock, I jumped up and down and wailed out loud and couldn't stop. I still don't know why my body and mind reacted that way, but maybe that was my dance of grief.

I was driven to the airport and boarded a plane home that day. I remember not being able to stop crying. My dad was my teacher with his words of wisdom, my coach in tennis and all sports, and my musician who taught me to sing. If I had my dad by my side, I knew everything would be okay. He was my rock, my stone.

Fountain Street Church was packed with more than one thousand people to mourn my father's passing. Since singing and music were one of our favorite shared moments together—my dad on his Martin guitar and me learning country songs by heart—I knew I needed to sing at his funeral. I chose "Take Me Home, Country Roads," as it was the first song I performed with my dad at age seven. I don't remember singing, just walking up to the front of the church and walking back down to my seat. In the shock I felt as if I was floating in a dream state. I could see the people, but I was not there. He was our sun, and now that the light had burned out, our family was scattered like planets no longer in orbit. We were each lost in our own grief, numb from our greatest loss.

The shock and disbelief from friends and family—that one of the top trial lawyers in the country had suffered from severe depression and taken his life—was impossible to comprehend. He was a man who most people thought had it all: brilliant, witty, charismatic, and a master of the English language. He would light up a room when he entered. He was a storyteller, a musician, a star athlete in his prime, a mentor and teacher, and a husband and father of three.

And with all of these amazing gifts came pride and the belief that he was alone. My dad was too proud to let the world know that he suffered from manic depression. Only our family and a few close friends knew how horribly he suffered and how hard he fought the darkness that was engulfing him. And he fought it like hell by admitting himself to the University of Michigan Hospital and taking antidepressants and finally the drug lithium. He once confided in me that it was like being in a dark hole, and you can't see your way out of it. At the time, I was young and unaware of the true depths of his pain, physically and mentally, that he was sinking into. I thought it was "just the blues" and it would pass as it always had, eventually. If I tiptoed around the house and was careful not to disturb him, he would come out of his bedroom and be okay again. I so wanted my dad to be okay and come back to us.

It has been thirty-four years since my dad lost his battle. If you live long enough, you are bound to have many highs and many lows, but nothing has rocked or changed my world as much as my father's suicide. It has shaped me in so many ways. The empathy I feel for others is profound, and I have found that forgiveness is the greatest gift you can give yourself and others. Every day is truly a gift, and to touch others' lives is what this life is all about.

I am the mother of three creative, loving, kind, and incredibly grateful children. They know their grandpa Mac was the world to me, and although they never knew him, through me they feel as if they had known him. I share stories about him, pass on his words of wisdom, and treasure when someone tells me they knew him. I hold on dearly to his few possessions that keep him close to me, and my children know that these treasures will someday be theirs. By sharing with my children all that I had with my dad, I have kept him alive. Suicide may have taken his body from us, but his spirit, or essence, is alive. I carry it with me.

Time has allowed me to understand that mental illness took my father's life. His pain from bipolar disorder had become unbearable, to the point that he could no longer go on.

That is what mental illness can do to the mind. It can make one truly believe that the world would be better off without them, and that the pain and suffering that they battle is too great to go on. My father may as well have had cancer of the brain that took his life.

He suffered from bipolar disorder associated with episodes of mood swings ranging from depressive lows to manic highs, which in his case produced suicidal thoughts and ultimately took his life.

It is only with greater acceptance and awareness that we can begin to understand that mental illness is a disease. It is a disease that has no cure. Only by talking and sharing our stories may we hope to touch someone who is battling mental illness and is seeing suicide as a way out.

A friend of mine fought mental illness and thoughts of suicide. He had been estranged from his daughter for several years, and after countless attempts to be in her life again, he became distraught to the point of not wanting to go on with his life. He was very close to taking his life and then remembered a conversation we had had a few years earlier, in which I shared how losing my dad to suicide was the most unimaginable loss for me—that my life had been shattered and I would never be the same again. It was in that moment my words came to him, and he chose not to take his life. Because I shared how suicide had impacted my life, not only did he realize he wasn't alone in his disease, but my words brought just a sliver of light into the darkness. He later told me I saved his life, and he wanted me to know. He told me that I was sunshine and needed to share it with others. That is when I realized the impact I could make for those suffering with mental illness.

My dad ran out of time, and the disease won. But it doesn't have to be that way today. We have come so far and will continue to battle this disease, until we win! Through educating ourselves and others by breaking the silence and stigma that goes along with suicide, we can succeed.

Today we can talk about suicide and pain and the anguish that comes with mental illness. We must share our stories, as it is the only way to help those who think they are all alone in their suffering.

NOT SO WONDERFUL LIFE

Losing a Father

Chase Woodrick

According to the ancient Chinese classic, *The I-Ching*, or *Book of Changes* in English, the different seasons found within nature represent far more than just the changing of the weather. They also represent the ever-changing phases of life that we humans go through.

In spring we see the plants slowly sprouting up from the ground, symbolizing birth and beginning. In the summer we have youthful, vigorous life, as we see that which sprouted in spring nearly comes to maturity. In autumn we receive nourishment, when we enjoy the fruits of our labor that have ripened. Winter is defined as a time of trial, a test, or an ordeal.

Reflecting on the power that separates what survives winter and what doesn't survive, I have always found this relationship between the seasons and life phases extremely relevant to myself. It is usually around the beginning of winter (the first week of November more specifically) that I find myself tested and tried in the severest of ways.

My first trial with winter was when I had to endure the abrupt loss of my father to suicide. It was more painful because it was the start of the holiday season, and I was bombarded with Hallmark images of perfect families coming together and celebrating with joy. I was so numb with pain that all this holiday cheer had a nauseating effect on me, as it conveyed a reality that was the opposite of mine.

I remember watching the holiday classic *It's a Wonderful Life*, and at the end, I wanted to throw my shoe through the television screen. It made me ask, *Where was my father's angel at his crucial hour of need when he needed sweet uplifting words to save his life?* Out for coffee, I guess.

So, during the holiday season, instead of getting carried away with the giving and receiving of neatly wrapped presents, why not look around for someone you know who is struggling through a harsh winter trial of their own, and give them the gift of compassionate understanding and unconditional love?

TALKING ABOUT THE DARKNESS

Losing a Father

Claire Anderson

My dad, Warren Eugene Anderson, died of suicide almost ten years ago, and not a day goes by that I don't think about him, how I lost him, and what could have been done differently. When I'm asked, "How did your dad die?" no one ever wants to hear the response "Suicide." People don't know how to respond, and it can be awkward. I want people to know suicide is a problem, and depression is a real issue! It should not be stigmatized or treated any differently than any other disease or health problem. We need to start conversations before it is too late.

My father was the first of his family to go to college and graduated with a degree from the University of Washington. He traveled the world and loved music and concerts, which he always took me to growing up. He would help anyone at the drop of a hat and loved working on his sports car. But most of all, his favorite thing in the whole world was being my dad. I know this because he would tell me every day, and he would also tell everyone he knew.

When I would meet his friends or coworkers they would say, "Your dad is so proud of you. He can't stop saying how much he loves you and how proud he is that you are his daughter." I would smile and nod, because I knew that he would even brag to me about me! He had so much love to share. He was at every single sporting event I had, and there were a lot! He taught me to play every sport out there since the time I could walk. We would spend weekends perfecting a new skill or making some new craft or project. He always had the best advice. He always said, "Don't have regrets. You made the best decision you could at the time." I live by that, knowing every day I am doing my best with the decisions and choices I make. We would talk every night on the phone, and as I grew up, every time I drove anywhere. I still pick up the phone to call him sometimes, forgetting he's no longer here. He never let a day go by without calling, telling me how much he loved me, and I know he is always there as my cheerleader and greatest support.

I lost my dad to suicide when I was twenty-one. For some reason, I always had a gut feeling that I would lose him this way. At a young age I would tell him to hold on and to just wait—things would get better. No child or adult should ever have that thought cross through their mind. He struggled with addiction and depression his whole life. There were good days and bad days. There were days when he was happy and joyful, which is how I always remember him, but also there were days when I knew he was struggling. It was hard when I was growing up because as a child I knew something wasn't right, but I could only do so much. I would try to make it better for him the best I could, making sure always to be happy around him and to spend as much time as I could with him. That was difficult sometimes as a growing teenager who would rather just hang with their friends than go hang with their dad on a Friday night. Sometimes when people are sick, you can try everything, but the illness is fatal.

When my dad died of suicide, no one really knew what to say or do. It was as if an illness or accident would have been more acceptable—people could understand that. It was hard for me to even say that suicide is how I lost my dad. I would try to explain it without saying the word, hoping that saying, "He was really depressed," would somehow make others feel better about hearing how he died. I'm not ashamed, but for some reason in society there is a stigma, a "don't speak about it" sort of thing, even though we all know it's nothing new.

It is not until you are personally affected by suicide that you actually begin to hear the little things people say to joke about suicide:

"Oh man, I just want to die"; "I would rather kill myself than do this"; or "Shoot me now." When I hear these things, I don't think anyone is actually grasping the magnitude of these statements. They don't seem to realize that someone around them may be actually feeling these things, or that someone hearing this may have actually lost someone that way. It is not until recently that I have started to speak up and let people know that we cannot joke about these things.

Because I work in the media, I am constantly hearing stories about suicide, depression, and mental-health issues. I have kept quiet about my experience, but every time I read a new story my heart breaks. It is not until recently that I have publicly shared my own experience with losing my dad to suicide.

In the summer of 2018, the media was filled with reports about the suicides of Avicii, Kate Spade, and Anthony Bourdain—all amazing, talented, and successful. The common thread was suicide. Everyone was shocked. *How could they commit suicide? They are so rich and have everything; life must be so amazing for them.* That's the secret of depression. It is sometimes the people you least expect. This is when I first shared publicly about what happened to my dad. I wanted the power back in my life story and wanted to let others know they are not alone.

My heart was breaking after learning that these talented people were gone too soon. I know suicide is not an easy topic to discuss, and no one is really comfortable bringing it up, but we need to be. Even saying the word can be difficult—trust me, I know.

Those losses in the media brought a dark subject and inner struggle into the light. Suicide happens to everyday people as well. I have also lost a dear friend to suicide while in college, and I am sure many other people know someone personally who has been affected by suicide. I hope that we can start talking about this issue, help those currently struggling, and prevent further loss in the future.

THE DANCE CONTINUES

Losing a Mother

Andrea Forsyth

On April 15, 2018, my mother lost a years' long battle with depression. Growing up, I always sensed that she was a bit "off." She could be moody, aloof, and cold, and she did not participate in life the way most people did. As a child and young woman, I internalized her behavior and always felt as if I had done something wrong. I was twenty-six years old when I finally recognized that the problem was not me; the problem was her worsening depression, which now included alcohol and prescription drug abuse. (Recognizing this was incredibly liberating, and it was at that point in my life that I began to thrive.) In 2013, my mom sent me an email describing the depression that was tightening its grip on her. She described a "total loss of zest for life" and a "weird or improper wiring in my brain."

My mom was struck by the sad irony of a song she used to love called "Those Were the Days" by Mary Hopkin. In that song, Hopkin laments catching her own reflection in the window of a tavern she used to frequent. She describes seeing a strange reflection and wondering whether that lonely woman was really her. After hearing that song, my mom said to me, "I didn't think those poignant lyrics would so dramatically relate to me. Unfortunately, I was wrong." In that same 2013 email, my mom wrote, "I truly look in the mirror sometimes and wonder, 'Where is that attractive, energetic person? What happened to that person, and can I ever get her back again?'"

My response was always, "Of course you can, but you need to try! You need to get help! Go for a run. Go to a yoga class. Meet a friend for lunch." These are the kinds of things that make me happy when I am feeling down, but I don't understand what it feels like to have a "total loss of zest for life" or an "improper wiring in my brain."

What I miss the most about my mom is her incredible potential. It is devastating that such a beautiful, intelligent, and successful woman was slowly lost to this terrible disease. After my mom's death, I received so many messages from her old friends and teachers. One of my favorites was from her former high school teacher whom she kept in touch with over the years. He described her as a "beyond beautiful young woman who seemed to excel at everything she did." That pretty much summed up my mom predepression. She was drop-dead gorgeous. She was funny and witty. She was athletic and smart. She graduated with honors from Albion College where she was the homecoming queen. She obtained a master's degree at the University of Michigan in the early 1970s when not a lot of women were doing that. She married a handsome and successful man and had two healthy children, who in turn provided her with five healthy grandchildren (and a sixth after her death).

My mom loved music. As a young woman, she spent her summers at her family's cottage, in Michigan on Torch Lake, where she worked as a singing cocktail waitress. She had a beautiful voice, and she loved to sing. She was always listening to her favorite albums from her generation, and she loved dancing around the house—or "boogie hopping," as she called it—with her grandchildren.

When I was a baby, she proclaimed ABBA's "Dancing Queen" as "our song." We danced to that song from my infancy through my adulthood. We danced to that song at my wedding, and I don't think I have ever seen her so happy. A few weeks before her death, I bought her a journal. A few days after her death, I found that journal and an entry inside that said, "Andrea, you are my Dancing Queen. I raised you to be a strong and independent woman, and in that I have succeeded."

My mom knew that her life looked perfect on paper, and she knew that she had a million things to be grateful for. Despite all of this, my mom became that lonely woman in the reflection. That beautiful and energetic person disappeared, and she never came back.

On April 15, 2018, my mom lost her battle with depression, although I didn't know that at the time. On that date, I was strolling through the French Quarter in New Orleans, blissfully unaware that my mom had passed away. Over the next three days, my phone calls and text messages went unanswered. On the morning of April 18, 2018, I awoke with an ominous feeling. My mom had struggled with depression and addiction issues for years, but in the weeks leading up to her death, her behavior had grown increasingly erratic. This, coupled with her radio silence, was deeply troubling. I remember that morning like it was yesterday. I exchanged text messages with my brother, who lives in Boston, and we agreed that I would go check on her. I didn't want to go by myself, so I called my close friend Samantha to meet me at my mom's house. I remember getting ready slowly and methodically, intentionally holding on to those last moments of a life uncomplicated by the searing grief that accompanies the loss of a mother. My heart knew that my mom was gone, but my head was not ready to accept that yet.

I dropped my children off at school and drove to my mom's house to meet Samantha and her father, who felt oddly compelled to be there. I am so grateful for that, as my own father was out of town at the time, and having him there provided great comfort. It was a beautiful, blue-skied, spring day, which was a juxtaposition to the scene that awaited us in the house where my mother lay dead from a self-inflicted gunshot wound. I will always remember April 18, 2018, as the day that my childhood home turned into a crime scene swarming with police officers and detectives, the day that it was transformed from a place of nostalgic comfort to a house of horrors that formed the backdrop of my nightmares for several months thereafter.

That awful day will haunt me for the rest of my life. But it was also the day that revealed infinite goodness in the hearts of my many friends. It was the day that my dear Samantha literally caught me when I fell and took control of an awful situation with such steely poise and grace. It was the day that my sweet Sara held me in her arms and stroked my back as I wept uncontrollably. It was a day at the forefront of many days to follow where my friends rallied around me with a constant stream of meals, gifts, hugs, and well-being checks.

In ways too complicated to explain here, my mother's death softened me. I have reconciled and made peace with a lot of dueling emotions. I learned that it is okay to be vulnerable, especially in the haven of friendship; vulnerability creates impenetrable strength and compassion and fosters an intimacy that cannot truly exist without it. I learned that strength and weakness are not mutually exclusive. During my mother's lifetime, her mental-health struggles caused our family a great deal of grief, and I carried around a lot of anger, resentment, frustration, and hurt. Now those negative emotions are gone, which has created extra space in my heart for the good ones.

My mom has been gone for five years now, and I have endured terrible grief and sadness. I have wept in the arms of good friends who have been pillars of strength for me when I could barely breathe. Some parts of the last few years have been awful, but some really great things have happened too—things that would make my mom so proud. I traveled to several bucket-list destinations. I continue to watch my beautiful children grow, and I have taken them on some fun adventures. My brother and his wife had their third daughter. My beloved dad found love and happiness with a woman whom we all adore (and, frankly, my mom would too). I completed my first Half Ironman. I made partner at my law firm. I won my first solo jury trial. My mom was a staunch feminist who always encouraged me to challenge myself personally and professionally. I will always remember her proudly exclaiming, "You go, girl! I am *so* proud of you!" at all of my accomplishments. I believe she continues to do so from above.

I know it might sound odd, but I believe that my mom speaks to me through music, which makes sense since we both love to sing.

In the days following her death, I listened to "Both Sides Now" by Joni Mitchell on repeat. I have heard that song a million times, but I did not really *hear* it until after she died. The lyrics of the first verse spoke to me so much so that I quoted them at her memorial. In that song, Mitchell describes a time in her life when she saw the clouds with optimistic delight and imagination, but eventually she stopped seeing them through this rose-tinted lens and they became nothing but dreary obstacles that got in the way of her happiness. To me, this verse aptly describes my mom's downward spiral into a depression that ultimately took her life.

My world was turned upside down after my mom's death. In the beginning, I questioned my ability to withstand such a tragedy. I feared that it would forever break me and dampen my fire. But it didn't. I am alive and whole and fiery as ever. Perhaps that's a testament to the strong and independent woman that my mom so proudly raised. My mom is at peace, and I will carry her with me on my life's journey. All the life experiences I accumulate along the way are her legacy.

Rest in peace, Mama. Your Dancing Queen lives on.

IT RUNS IN THE FAMILY

Generational Pain

Andrea S.

My journey started in the winter of 2016. During this time of year, we're aware that seasonal depression can gripe us at any moment, but I wasn't ready for what was ahead. My husband started a new job earlier that year, leaving a career he was comfortable with for something that was a bit more challenging but also rewarding.

It was a few weeks before Christmas when it began. He wasn't his usual self, and by that, I mean he seemed off. He backed away from all our normal holiday activities, which included decorating the tree, shopping for presents for the kids, and baking cookies. Then he started saying that I would be better off without him and that he didn't belong here. I remember he was sitting on our bed, and I sat on the floor asking him what was going on. Was it stress, anxiety, too much going on at work? Could I be of help?

I suggested he give his doctor a call and left it at that. About a week later, things got much worse. He slept on the couch and didn't want to go to work. I kept trying to get him moving, but no luck. I told him to call his boss and take the day off work, and we'd talk again when I got home. I'm not sure what it was about that day, but I was afraid to leave him home alone.

I decided to go to work and figured I should keep everything as normal as possible, and if the kids asked what was wrong, I was going to just tell them, "Dad isn't feeling well." During the last couple of years, mental health was starting to become a topic that was being talked about more and more. I realized all the signs were there pointing to someone who needed help, and I just kept pushing them away.

I needed to be the one to make that first difficult call to get him help. That's when I picked up the phone and called our mental-health services. I locked myself in our half bathroom because I didn't want him to hear me calling. My hands were shaking, I was scared, and tears were welling up in my eyes. Was I imagining things? Was I making a poor decision? Maybe he was "okay"? I was able to get him in for an evaluation in a couple of weeks.

Between that phone call and his appointment, he hit rock bottom. One night he went outside on the deck and kept looking down. It looked like he was going to jump down from it at any moment. I was screaming at him to come inside and walk away and that everything would be fine. I had just put the kids to bed and prayed that they weren't going to wake up. While my gut told me to call 911, I just couldn't do it. I called my mother-in-law instead. Why choose her in that moment? I remember my husband telling me that his mom had been through a dark time in her life, too, and when he was little she was hospitalized for depression and anxiety. He was just told she was "sick" and would be better soon. I don't think he had understood the gravity of it or that one day he would be going through the same thing. She said at one point she had planned to end her life but by divine intervention was saved. After she arrived, we finally got him to relax and got him to our room, where he fell asleep. I made another call, and we were able to move up his appointment.

When he finally got in and was evaluated, they kept him for a long time. I don't think I heard from him until just around dinnertime. The therapist and doctors thought he was going to harm himself and wanted to take him to the hospital right away, but he kept telling them he wanted to be with his family for Christmas, which was a few days out. They did give him permission to come home, but he was put into a partial hospitalization program, which was to start right after the holidays were over. I know the first day of treatment was the hardest for him, but slowly with the help of his counselors he was able to start training his mind to "think" in another way.

They also recommend medication for him, which he was very against. He thought it was going to change him and he would have to take these pills for his entire life. I helped him recognize that if he had cancer or another illness, he'd take medicine for that, so how was this any different? After treatment, medication, and regular check-ins, I could tell it was as if this heavy burden had been taken away from him.

In no way is this a permanent fix. He still has some bad days, but they're sprinkled in with a lot of happier days now. During that time, I also told my coworkers that my husband tried to end his life. I wanted to be open about it and did end up taking some time off as well. Through this whole ordeal I don't think I really ever fully told our kids what was going on. Maybe I didn't know how I was going to explain it at the time, and I didn't want them to feel the weight of it, either.

However, my story doesn't end here. I've always said my daughter got the best of both of us. She's smart and funny like my husband and athletic, caring, and compassionate like me. She didn't become a big sister until just before she turned five. My husband and I spent every moment with her, taking her on adventures to the park, golfing, and ice skating. Then the boys were born eighteen months apart, and life got crazy. She has grown up with lots of friends, she played soccer with a local league, and like any child she had a zest for life. Midway through elementary school we moved to a new house, changed school districts, and started to become more involved in our community. Our daughter was doing well in school, always received glowing compliments from her teachers, and started taking up new hobbies, including playing a musical instrument and painting. One of the best parts of parenting is seeing your child become more independent and finding out what their interests are. She found a new group of friends and even started going to summer camp with them.

While our daughter has always been shy and reserved at times, once you get her talking it is always hard to stop her. It wasn't until middle school started that we noticed changes. She started putting pressure on herself to do well in school, even though we told her we just wanted her to try her best, regardless of the outcome, and we'd be proud of her no matter what. Also during this time more of her teachers were requiring students to give presentations in front of the class. This made her so anxious that she'd come home crying, saying, "I just can't do it," and when she did try to give a presentation, she'd start crying and run out of the room. She was always worried about what her peers would think of her after these episodes. We were always able to calm her down and said to just keep trying and eventually it would get better. We did go to the school counselor and told her about our daughter's anxiety and how she was having a hard time speaking in front of her classmates. The counselor understood and made her office a safe space for her to go if she needed it. Some teachers were even kind enough to let her give her presentations to them before school started, so she could still be graded.

I'm not sure how this day was different from any others. She had been working on a speech all week for a class and assured us she was ready to go, but while I was at work that morning, I received a phone call that she wasn't in school. I kept thinking about all the bad things that could have happened to her. I tried calling her phone and received no answer. I hysterically called my husband and raced home.

I found her in her bedroom, crying, shaking, and saying she just couldn't do it. I hugged her and told her we'd get some more help. It was at this point that we started taking her to an outside counselor. It was a blessing. She started to learn a few techniques that could help her calm down, and the counselor recommended journaling to release her thoughts. After about a month or so, we noticed progress and slowly stopped her appointments.

For high school our daughter decided to go to a smaller school. It turned out to be a great choice because of the smaller class sizes and more one-on-one opportunities with the staff. Her first year of high school was during the pandemic. She was taking virtual classes for a while, and after the holidays she was able to go back to in-person learning. She did talk to her school counselors and teachers about how talking in front of the class made her nervous, and they were all supportive and said she could come talk to them at any time. During the spring, she made the varsity soccer team and gained more friends. A few weeks before the season was over, she injured herself and was out for the rest of the season. She continued to go to all their games and ended on a high note.

Even in such a crazy pandemic year of uncertainty, she finished with straight As and lots of memories. Summer started, and we had a doctor's appointment scheduled to get her athletic form filled out for the next school year. It was at this appointment that our pediatrician pulled me aside after, asking if I knew that our daughter was feeling more and more anxious about life in general and suggesting that maybe it would be best to start taking her back to the counselor she had seen a couple of years ago. In the car on the way home I asked her why she didn't tell me she was feeling anxious and sad. She said she didn't want to bother us about it because both of us were stressed out with our jobs and figuring out summer plans.

I reminded her that communication is key, and she takes priority over everything else. She said she understood, and I thought everything was good. We made an appointment midsummer with the counselor, and after a few sessions, I thought we were on the right path again. One night I was waiting for her session to be over, thinking we'd make another appointment for the following week and head home for dinner, but the counselor asked to talk to me privately. She told me my daughter was in rough shape and we needed to take a bigger leap.

The counselor told me my daughter was thinking about taking her own life, and her mind kept taking her to the medicine cabinet. She had told her counselor that she wanted me to lock up all the medication in the house to prevent her from doing anything.

My heart sank so fast, and even though I wanted to cry, I remained calm. If I learned anything from the last few years, it's that panicking doesn't help the situation.

My daughter, the pediatrician, and I together decided it would be in her best interest to do to partial hospitalization as we had done with my husband. When we got home, I told him everything, and he was devastated. He didn't want her to be going through the same thing he did. Why did she have to be feeling this way? He was so upset that he locked himself in the bathroom that night and fell asleep on the floor.

I once again made the call to our local mental-health services facility, this time for my daughter. The night before she started her treatment, we sat down after dinner and told her this would be one of the hardest things she'd ever do, but it was an important step in having the "pain" that she kept describing to us go away.

Her sessions got underway; she would be there for a week. The first day she met with her health team, and she did just fine. As the week went on it did get harder, but she said she was thankful for other teens in her group who "understood" how she felt. During the week the parents and child meet for a couple of hours to talk about how things are going and what the next steps are after the child is released. Those two hours were almost unbearable for me. My daughter told us she was hiding her feelings from us still because she didn't want to be a burden. She also described the "pain" again and how she wanted it to go away. She thought overdosing on medication would be her answer, or jumping off the bridge that's near our house, but she knew she could never do it.

I had a lump in my throat, and tears started to well up in my eyes. The doctor asked us if we had noticed any signs, and looking back, they were right in front of us. I really thought she was just being a teenager by sleeping in on summer mornings and just hanging out in her room. But what I missed was that she wasn't inviting friends over, even when we said she could, her art canvases were blank this summer, and she didn't want to spend time with her family, including her brothers.

When we left the office, my husband asked if that whole conversation reminded me of anything. He said it was like looking at himself all over again.

She's now on medication and will continue to seek help from her counselors. She has a long journey ahead of her with her mental illness and anxiety. It will never just go away, but over time she'll learn more about how her brain works, what triggers her anxiety and fears, and how she can cope with it. I'm forever grateful that my husband and daughter are still here, and I know I'm one of the lucky ones.

I want people to know we need to continue to talk about mental health; we need to wrap our arms around those going through depression or anxiety and let them know they're not alone. To anyone reading this, know that you are strong enough to help someone through it. Some days may be tough, tears will fall, and you'll wonder, "Why me?"—but know that you're saving a beautiful life.

LIFE WITH GRIEF AND DEPRESSION

Losing a Spouse and Parents

Chris VanZee

When my husband died, I thought it would be the hardest moment of my life, but it was only the beginning of a nightmare and a total transformation of who I am today.

It started on a day like any other: the kids were off to work and school, and my husband, Chuck, was off to work as well. I had made him promise to call his doctor that day, as he had a chest cold and wasn't getting much better. He fought me on seeing the doctor since it was a busy time at work and he didn't want to leave them short-handed. I don't recall what I was doing that day, except that I was at home. I had closed my childcare business that had kept me busy for almost twenty years, and I really didn't need to work anymore. I called Chuck that afternoon to see what his doctor had said; he received a couple of medications and was sent back to work. Within an hour of this conversation he arrived home and said the guys at work made him leave since he was feeling so lousy. I remember every minute of what was to follow because it is engrained in my brain forever.

He had his newly filled prescriptions in hand and some fast food when he walked in the door. He was having a hard time eating and talking and took a puff of an inhaler that he had just picked up from the pharmacy. I have some medical training, and I couldn't believe his doctor didn't do more for him. I suggested we take him to the ER because it was so hard for him to breathe. Chuck normally was quite a baby when sick, but he said, "No, I just want to go downstairs and watch TV." Chuck had had asthma his whole life, but it never really bothered him much in his adult years. I assumed he would know if he needed to be checked out.

Chuck went downstairs and I went about what I was doing; only about five minutes later, he yelled for me. He said he was getting worse, so I told him it was time to go in to the ER. He didn't think he would be able to make it up the stairs. I was shocked, so at this point we decided to call 911 for assistance. The paramedics came quickly, asked him multiple questions, started treating him, and decided to take him in. They struggled getting him up the stairs; that was frustrating me—I just wanted them to give him some relief. He was breathing very hard again and they promised to give him another breathing treatment soon. Once they were on the front sidewalk, he was able to stand and get on the gurney, and they loaded him into the ambulance. I had planned to follow; I quickly grabbed his coat and shoes along with my keys, and we were on our way.

The paramedics were driving at a normal pace with me following, but as soon as they hit the highway, they turned on the lights and sirens and took off. I wasn't sure whether I was allowed to drive that fast, so I went quickly but couldn't quite keep up. I was calling a couple of our kids to tell them that we were on our way to the hospital, but not to worry—he probably needed some proper meds or had pneumonia. I promised to provide updates. As I arrived and walked into the emergency room and gave Chuck's name, they told me to take a seat. *Weird*, I thought, *wouldn't they just show me to what cubicle he was in?* A social worker came to talk to me and said they were currently working on him; she would see if the doctor was available to update me. She moved me back to a hallway in the ER area. I didn't think much of it but assumed they were busy trying to figure things out.

When a doctor came down the hall he told me that things weren't going well and that Chuck's heart had stopped on the way to the hospital; they were having trouble getting it going. *What did he say? Did he have the right person?* My brain skipped a gear—stopped computing. My medical mind was saying, This is not good, but yet I couldn't make sense of the doctor's words. *Is this man telling me Chuck is dying?* In a normal state I would have known how dire this situation was; I just listened and sat there stunned.

The doctor asked whether I wanted to come in to Chuck's room. I saw people running in and out of the room and said, "I don't want to be in the way." I think I was horrified to face what was happening and thought they would fix Chuck if I stayed out of the way. I don't think my feet could have moved, but the next thing I knew, someone was guiding me in there anyway. I was mortified at seeing them doing chest compressions, seeing his face. I kept saying over and over again, "THIS IS NOT HAPPENING, THIS IS NOT REAL." I remember a nurse rubbing my back as I sat there staring but not really seeing or believing what I saw.

The doctor said there was one more thing they could try, and I said, "Yes, please." Then I said a quick prayer: "Please, God, let this work." I told Chuck, "Hon, hang on. We love you and need you." Somehow I was escorted back to the hall and they put my chair right outside his room. I couldn't breathe, couldn't think. I was frozen, perhaps in shock. People handed me tissues. I wasn't crying—was I supposed to be crying? Were they going to think I was uncaring if I wasn't crying? How was I supposed to be acting? So many thoughts but my brain was just not working properly. I don't even know if I could have come up with my full name if asked.

At some point the doctor came out of the room and said they had to stop compressions. I just sat there. I knew what this meant. I felt like a bad person because my first thought was, *Oh my God, where will we live? How can I keep a roof over my kids' heads? Are we going to be homeless?* I think my brain was trying to go into survival mode. The kind social worker appeared and asked whom to call. Seriously in shock, I couldn't think of anyone. She finally found out that we had children and got a phone number for my daughter. My kids came one by one, and it was a night of disbelief and shock. Each one of them seemed to be affected in different ways, handling it with their own brain's and heart's capacity. I hugged and clung to the one crying the most—but maybe one of the others needed more attention; I didn't know. There were no lessons in life for dealing with such things.

Fast forward to life beyond the services. This is the time when most people are deep in the trenches of grief. Not this girl—I was scared to death about taking care of my family. I sought financial planners and started desperately searching for work that I could do to help sustain the level of living the kids and I were accustomed to. My youngest was a senior in high school, and his prom was just a couple weeks after the funeral, so I threw myself into mom mode: getting a tux and everything else he'd need to wear and promising I'd get a limo for him and his friends. I couldn't afford the expenses at the time, but I felt the need to keep my promise because my son had just lost his dad.

My son's graduation and open house, all the lasts of a senior year, were coming up. I had so much to do on top of all the paperwork involved after a spouse passes away. I was overwhelmed with putting one foot in front of the other to keep life as normal as possible for my poor kids. They were my priority—no time for tears. I received many comments on my strength and brave face, but moving forward and keeping things as normal as possible seemed to be the only way I could breathe. I didn't know any other way. Over time, this was not the best for my mental health, but I also learned that the brain does what it does as a coping mechanism. Marching forward, being the strong mom, kept me grounded in order to do what I was doing.

After we got through those first few months and had a few special events without Chuck, I started working and making a financial plan; I was a robot. I realized that as much as I tried to keep everything going as it had been, life was never going to be the same for any of us again. More tears flowed than they had in the initial days after Chuck's death, when I would stop them in their tracks. I remember thanking God every day for the years we had Chuck in our lives and the memories we shared. Nothing could take those away, but I would still feel sorrow over being a widow in my forties. Then I would thank God that at least I still had my kids. They were and are my everything.

I would do everything in my power to love my kids and give them everything I could. They each were affected so differently in ways unique to their personality and relationship with their father. I understood most of them, but not all. They didn't always understand me either, which also caused problems later on. I didn't seek any help with grief initially. I didn't think I needed help and didn't have the time for it. I did shed tears at times, and I was beginning to know how a date or song could easily trigger deep feelings from within. As the first holidays without Chuck approached, I knew it was in my best interest to seek counseling because I wanted to be prepared. I had no idea how the holidays would affect me or the kids. One constant throughout was that I always wanted to do the best thing for all of us. My youngest was already starting to suffer from depression. I had been diagnosed with PTSD. I knew it was important to take care of our mental health, but none of us had issues with it before, and I didn't think mental-health issues would just start up due to a single event.

I didn't know where to go for help. Someone recommended a place that had small groups and was free of charge. Many in my group described how I felt with 100 percent accuracy, and it was great to be validated in the feelings I was having. I learned that grief affects us all differently, depending on one's personality and the closeness of relationship to the person who died. I was a strong person, not the one to wallow in self-pity and curl up in a ball in my room with tears for days. I prided myself on being strong for my kids. I didn't want them to worry about their mom after losing their dad; I was going to be the rock. I wanted them to know we would all be okay and get through this together.

I was constantly pouring myself into things I could do to honor my kids' dad, especially on those days that had special meaning. This was healing for me, and I thought I was doing something important for my kids and my husband. I did well for a while but finally sought more counseling as I struggled with more difficulties on a personal level. The biggest one for me was, Where have all our friends gone? The ones Chuck and I had seen regularly were out having good times without me. I saw it all over Facebook but never got my invite. I felt as if they didn't care anymore. They all expect you to get over it and be fun to be around. A close friend said to me a few months after my husband's passing, "What's wrong with you?" *Really?* I thought. I choked back tears behind my sunglasses and walked away. I wanted to scream, "My husband, my kids' father, is gone—forever—along with all our future plans and dreams. GONE!" I went through a time of feeling lost and alone; no one seemed to understand. I focused on my kids and getting myself to counseling regularly. I was not feeling as strong as I once was, but I was still doing okay.

Next, my dad died almost as suddenly and unexpectedly as Chuck had. I didn't grieve him either; I just kept busy with life. I cried, sure, but not for long, and I felt that the loss of Chuck was always in the forefront. My dad had stepped up to take care of the many guy things that I needed help with since Chuck's passing, and now he was gone as well. My brain handled this loss as well as the ones yet to come in the same way. I told myself, *Just keep going, be strong, and don't think about it. Just keep moving forward.*

I had to start selling pieces of our old life out of necessity—everything Chuck and I had worked hard to have: our beautiful home, our vacation place up north. It was like selling off parts of my heart and soul. I knew it was the financially smart thing to do, so I had to be brave and keep going. *So many people have to do this*, I told myself. *It's part of life. Don't be a baby. You are strong.*

My counselor had warned me about handling things in this way, and boy, did I learn the hard way. Lesson number one was don't set your grief aside for later. Setting my grief aside was what suited me at the time, and my body and brain learned that it worked as a response to coping with overwhelming grief and loss. When tears crept in,

I would tell myself, *Not now*. I kept stuffing my feelings in a vault, as my counselor called it, and then one day the vault could handle no more. The hinges blew off that door and I fell apart—badly. I now was diagnosed with depression for the first time in my life. I thought I knew what depression was when my son was diagnosed. I had heard of others having it. I thought it was just the feeling of being sad and not knowing how to feel better. I don't think anyone can actually understand depression until you actually have it yourself. Now I know how debilitating it is. I couldn't stop crying, couldn't get out of bed, couldn't go to work. It was awful, and I was scared.

I tried natural remedies, but my depression was too bad, and they weren't helping. I knew I had to go to the doctor. I couldn't even make the appointment without crying. My youngest was the only one living at home now, and he saw the state I was in. Since he had suffered with depression after the loss of his dad, he understood what I was going through. I remember crying hard and apologizing to him for not understanding his depression better. There were days I had thoughts of not wanting to be here anymore. Those scared me so bad. I cried like a baby. Where did that strong rock who didn't wallow in tears go? Where was the person who would never curl up in a ball and just lie there? I was no longer that girl. Since I was alone a lot, I grew very afraid of it and didn't want to be alone. I reached out to friends and my mom whenever I felt alone. It was a distraction and a crutch to help pass the time and ease the horrible feelings of loss and loneliness. I especially did this when I had feelings of not wanting to be here anymore. I now realize that my fear of being alone also stemmed from all of this. So now I have an intense need to talk to someone until the feelings get better. Before I stuffed them in a vault; now that the vault is broken, I have a different coping mechanism.

I fought hard to get back to being me. Lots of counseling and medications helped so much, but I had to learn that I had no identity anymore. How would I live a life different from what I had envisioned? I took many grief classes, too, and focused on getting back to who I thought I was or should be. It was three years after the loss of Chuck, and I felt so misunderstood during this time. There were many who didn't understand depression: "Why are you crying and a mess *now*?" I was judged for saying I had PTSD, for taking meds, for going to counseling. Even my own kids thought I was faking it (besides the son who lived with me). So with the loss of my kids having faith in me, I fell even deeper. I felt more alone and was terrified of it. I still hate being alone today.

I finally worked my way off the medications and felt that things were going great in my life. Then my mom, who was in great health, suddenly contracted a rare disease that destroyed her brain quickly. She went from living alone and working out at the gym to rapidly declining and passing away within five weeks before we could even figure out what was going on. It was yet another stunning loss that we couldn't comprehend or prepare for. I stuffed my grief aside even though I knew I should not. My brain has been rewired to do it that way because it worked for me in the past. *When will I grieve my mom?* I didn't know. I was executor of her estate and again was thrown into so many responsibilities. I sought counseling again, and thank God I have friends and a wonderful man in my life whom I could vent to and confide in.

I still have troubles today. I still call my counselor when I feel the need and reach out to friends at the drop of a hat. I know I am damaged from all these traumatic events, and I cry very easily. Things affect me deeply. Relationships with my kids or others can be difficult because they don't understand. I am not the person I was before these losses and never will be again. In many ways I am so much better, though. I have a heart that loves harder and deeper. I have a sense of compassion that greatly exceeds what I had in the past—and I thought that was a lot. I will continue to work on me because I'm important, and I know I have great things to contribute. I hope my story helps someone to understand that grief is different for each of us and that it's always a good idea to seek help. I also hope that it will help those who are blessed to not have any experience with this type of loss or mental illness. Please don't judge. Have a heart; ask questions. I know it's hard to understand, but it is devastating and not what any of us wants to live with, even for a day.

Now you see why the loss of my spouse may not have been the most difficult moment of my life, but the days, months, and years to follow have been tough on me due to that moment in time. My life was forever changed in a moment—in one breath. I will forever miss Chuck and my parents, but I'm so blessed to have had them in my life for as long as I did. Never take a day for granted with your loved ones. I have learned some valuable lessons through loss and am constantly changing and evolving into the best person I can be. God has a plan for all of us, and I feel peace in knowing I'm right where I belong and he will never leave my side. Peace to you all.

LOSS OF A LOVED ONE

Losing a Spouse

Vonnie Woodrick

Since the passing of my husband almost twenty years ago, life isn't what I expected it to be. After all these years, so much grief and sadness still linger throughout my days and my nights. Don't get me wrong—I consider myself a happy person, or maybe *content* is a better word. Love surrounds me in all different forms from all different places. That makes me happy, yet something is missing.

I don't mind being single, but I do mind being a widow. I never imagined a life without my spouse, and being forced to live life without him has been quite the adjustment. It's hard to believe that my kids have now lived longer without their dad than with their dad. I can't help but wonder, *What would they be like if he was still here? How different would our life be, and what path would each of them be on?* The unexpected death of a loved one is both shocking and devastating, and the pain never really goes away. In some way, I think the pain deepens.

I do know that the only way to get through any challenge in life is through acceptance. Acceptance sucks. Yet, if I didn't accept his death, I worry about what I would become. Not getting out of bed, perhaps self-medicating, or going days without showering are all possibilities. Those things are what pain does to us, and not accepting what life throws at you only increases the pain that could lead to depression, anxiety, and who knows what else.

Acceptance doesn't come quickly. Acceptance is a process. I've heard over and over again, "Accept the things you cannot change." Although that's a tough request, it's what we need to do to move forward.

As life moved forward, I know I became more anxious about things I never worried about before the death. I became an anxious person. I'm sure to all those around me I appeared to have it all together and handled life with gusto. Although I was the widowed person raising three kids alone, I was always the one others turned to when they had a problem or an issue that they needed advice on.

When that call came in and someone needed me, I felt valued. It was my high. Maybe I believed that I went through everything I went through in order to help others—a justification for all the pain.

It took me a long time to realize that I wasn't getting back what I was giving out. The friends who called and needed support weren't there for me when I needed a shoulder to cry on. My cup was becoming empty. I was doing a great job of letting everyone believe just how fine I was. But I wasn't fine.

I became depressed. I didn't want to get out of bed. I cried in the shower and wondered, *How did I ever get here?* You know the very basic question we all ask when we see one another, "How are you?" We generally answer, "I'm good, how are you?" When friends asked me how I was, I started to change up my answer and told several friends, "I'm not doing well." Every single one of them had a different response, and the responses weren't what I expected or wanted. I may have gotten the "You will be fine" or "At least the sun is out" response, which didn't help me.

Most often they would turn the tables and start talking about their own issues. I felt dismissed, discounted, and alone, even though I had been a cheerleader for them.

When you're in a depressed state, it doesn't matter if the sun is out; it takes a lot of energy to go for that thirty-minute walk that is supposed to change your mood. I knew I had to do something, but I didn't know what or how to change how I was feeling. I was the strong one—the one who never appears to be weak because she stays home and finds excuses to avoid being surrounded by everyone else who appears to be happy.

I don't mean to be a downer here, but every single day is still hard.

There are little reminders every day that life isn't what it was supposed to be or what I wanted it to be. We all have dreams—don't we? I often ask the questions, *Why are my kids the ones who had to grow up without their dad? Why am I a widow? Why did he have to go? What would he look like now? Who would we all be?*

Life as a single person in a couples' world is challenging. Being invited to a party alone isn't easy.

With no plus-one (most often I don't have one), I walk into a room full of friends who are with their spouses. Knowing life didn't change for them, but life changed for me, isn't easy. My life with my husband in it flashes before me. *What if he was here?* They were "our" friends, friends as couples. Most often, I don't get invited to such events. I see pictures of dinner celebrations, birthday parties, and couples' trips. I am no longer included, and I can't help but wonder, *Is it me? Did I do something? Did they only invite us because of my husband? Or is it because I am single and no longer fit in the couple category?*

The wedding invite is a whole other level of triggering emotions and images of what was supposed to be. I once received an invitation to a wedding, as the daughter of friends of both my husband and me was getting married. I was so excited to attend, knowing I would have several friends attending too. The wedding itself was more emotional than I anticipated, watching the father of the bride walk his daughter down the aisle, which hit me like a tsunami. I felt tears well up, then flow; then I couldn't breathe. I needed to get a grip. As I sat down, I raced my mind with other thoughts, trying to make myself believe that I wasn't really there. I was glad when that was over. I proceeded to the reception, by myself in my own car.

I arrived at the reception and made small talk with friends as we awaited the arrival of the bride and groom. We walked into the country club, were handed a glass of champagne, and got our seat assignments. I was at table one. *Wow, table one—what did that mean?* I was feeling pretty special, thinking I was perhaps at a special table. Well, table one was in the corner in the back of the ballroom, and I sat with strangers. I knew no one. I guess that is what happens when you are a single—they put you where there is one extra seat.

It may sound a bit petty, to feel rejected as a single person, sitting at a table with no one you know, yet being surrounded by tables of friends who are all laughing, toasting, and eating together. Again, so much crossed my mind. I felt as if I had lost my husband all over again. I knew, if he was there, we would be celebrating with friends, not with strangers. I felt as if I couldn't breathe and just wanted to get out, with a flood of emotions wanting to burst out of me.

I sat and watched the father and mother of the groom beaming with pride. It was a happy time for everyone except maybe for me. I was happy for them; I just wasn't happy for me. I kept contemplating my exit plan, searching for just the right moment to escape what seemed like an eternity. The band started right away with an announcement—asking those who have been married for fifty years or more to come on the dance floor, followed by twenty-five years and downward. That was almost too much for me, and I escaped. So many happy couples were still together after all these years. That would never be me. I left, and I cried all the way home.

There are many situations that can trigger grief—and, boy, was I triggered. So many emotions came pouring in that I had to get out. So much has changed since my husband's death, and all the special days, holidays, and events aren't the same. The loss is tremendous, and all these years later, the pain still lingers, and triggers are real.

This situation is one example from my years of experiencing life as a widow. Every day on social media, you see happy couples out with each other—posts with captions such as "My man," or "Blessed to have had thirty years, looking forward to thirty more," or "Don't know what I would do without them." Each time, it's a little sting, a sting that keeps coming back.

You would think, after all these years, those things wouldn't bother me. Yet it's those things that remind me of what could've been. I think about the parents who have lost a child, seeing every classmate, every friend, and every relative live life as a whole family. Being reminded of what was supposed to be is tough, really tough— heartbreaking to say the least.

Let's go back to acceptance. I have accepted my life's journey. It's just different from what I planned. Does that make it bad? No. It just makes it different. I have found that expressing gratitude for all the things I do have has helped. I realize there are so many in this world who are better off than I am, but there are so many more who aren't. I think that's what really drives me: truly knowing that pain exists in all our lives, yet some hurt so much more than others. Some pain goes away, but some is here to stay, sometimes for a lifetime.

Gratitude allows me to see that even though my life isn't what I dreamed of, it's still good. The accomplishments I've experienced are what make me most proud. These accomplishments go far beyond being a published author, podcast host, or founder of a nonprofit organization. They include the times when I am seeing my kids doing the right things, watching them growing up without a dad and being okay, seeing the world beyond things, truly appreciating time as being precious, and understanding that love heals. Those are the accomplishments that aren't seen by many but are felt by me and for which I have the most gratitude.

In my mind I often go back to the different chapters of my life. Most seem to be bittersweet. I think about everything that I went through, including being punched in the stomach as a child in first grade, which landed me in the hospital for an appendix removal— today the scar is still there. I made it through, yet I was scarred for life because of someone else's decision to be a bully.

Every one of our life experiences brings us to where we are supposed to be. I had to go through every single bittersweet moment to appreciate all the good moments, and that is just what they are sometimes: moments that will stay with you for a lifetime. A moment can change your course of direction. A moment can be worth every pain. I live for moments. I appreciate moments. I am grateful for moments.

Accepting my journey, expressing gratitude for everything I have, and appreciating moments shared with others are the most precious gifts I can give myself. I give these gifts to myself to remind myself that although life isn't what I planned for me, there was a bigger plan that brought me things I never knew I needed—such as purpose, rewards, and love from unexpected places.

Finding your purpose gives you a reward. What is your purpose in your life? If you don't know, then you haven't experienced life at its fullest. What is the reason you get up in the morning? Why do you do what you do, beyond the paycheck?

Once you discover your purpose, reap the rewards—it is then that you will find your true calling. The love you receive from unexpected places is just that: unexpected. Maybe it's the hug from a stranger, or a note in the mail, or someone simply smiling and opening the door for you. Those are the small things that mean the most. Those are the things that, when discovered, open a whole new world to acceptance and understanding.

JOY RE-CREATED

Losing a Spouse

Terry Jelsema

Following the death of my wife, Marlys, in 2019, I became acutely aware of the sheer heaviness of grief. It was all-encompassing: it enveloped my mind, became part of my body, and fractured my soul. The darkness was like nothing I ever experienced or felt before. It was a gut punch that resonated to the core of my being.

In brief moments of reflection, I wondered if I could ever escape grief's grip. Would I ever feel happiness or joy again?

But how does one assume that by sitting in grief long-term, by rolling in it, by making a bed in it, this by itself will bring about healing? I spent so much time in this space. Too much time was spent in this place! I couldn't get out of my own head.

Can sorrow alter sorrow's trajectory? Do I actually have a choice to be happy? Am I welded to grief, or do I have the dynamic ability to move away from grief toward joy?

The more I live in a sorrowful place, the dark dungeon of my mind, the less light I am able to appreciate. Grief held my face away from the cave opening. It applied metaphorical horse blinders to me, lessening the likelihood of my experiencing any light of joy. Everything had shades of gray and black. There was no color, no vibrancy to life. I grasped for the shadow of the life I had before. Joy became alien to me. The brightness and the sensation of positive emotions became foreign and unobtainable. I ran from joy. I hid from it. I feigned a false smile so that others would think I was experiencing joy.

Mind you, I do believe that joy and sorrow can cohabitate. I do not diminish the impact or the power of grief. I do not minimize that in the first year or two the darkness of grief is palpable, and the pinpoints of light or joy are minimal to nonexistent. Yet as time goes on, I have the choice of living in the dungeon of my mind, tortured by pain, or leaving that cell. There is no jailer; there are no guards. I just need to be courageous and walk through the mouth of the cave back into light.

I felt grief was indomitable at times. It conceived in me feelings of depression, anxiety, hopelessness, and helplessness. At times I felt these emotions crystallized like granite inside me. They were smelted from the heat of mortality. They seemed to stay fiery hot for so long, I thought they would never be able to cool. When these emotions did cool, they formed coarse edges, which continued to cause discomfort and tears. Through this fiery entanglement of raw emotions, however, the edges started to blunt and the coarseness began to diminish after some time and processing.

It took me a year and a half before I started seeking and seeing daylight, before I could appreciate joy even in its most elemental form. I needed to learn to be gentle on myself while I grieved. Self-judgment was a surefire way to keep me in the darkness.

My premise is that sorrow likes sorrow, and grief likes grief. But sorrow cannot be healed through more sorrow; grief cannot be softened by more grief. Sorrow has to be altered in joy. I think sorrow can be changed through joy. The true power of joy is its transformational power to puncture small holes into the darkness of grief and sorrow. Every time joy is experienced, grief becomes softer, less intense. Joyful feelings lessen the grip and control of grief over my life. Each moment of joy changes my perspective: it changes my taste, the sensation of my fingertips, and the light that penetrates my globes. It gives me a little more of a toehold, a handhold in this new world without my spouse.

Again, sorrow has its own gravitational force. Sometimes, it makes life so heavy that I believe I'm on another planet. Joy changes that gravitational force; it normalizes that gravitational pull and allows me to lift myself out of the dirt to stand in a new place, a higher place, with a fresher perspective. I can choose joy, and I have the power to allow it into my darkest places. In fact, I need it to punctuate my darkest places.

I have always envisioned that joy is a destination or at minimum a goal. Who doesn't want to be joyful in life? I set up joy as a goal no differently than I set up five-year business plans. I told myself that I'd reach such an age, and I would be joyful. I told myself that if I reached such a level of financial security or had x number of dollars in the bank, I would have joy. I expected that in my old age Marlys and I would have found joy together as we continued to mentor our children and grandchildren, even our great-grandchildren. Joy was written in each one of those goals—maybe in invisible ink, but it still was written on the parchment of our charter.

What I have found is that joy has to be pursued; it has to be created. It can even be re-created for those of us who feel that joy will never revisit us. I find joy in walking down a sidewalk and feeling the wind, snow, and rain hit my face. I can see a monarch butterfly dance before me, the delicate minute flowers of Queen Anne's lace, or hear the waves rhythmically hitting the shoreline. These all bring a smile, an adjustment to center, and allow me to reflect on something other than the gnarled feelings between my ears. Out of these types of events, joy is constructed.

What I mean by that is, if I set my butt on a chair all day (metaphorical for me sitting on the pity pot), I could talk myself out of doing anything that could expose me to the beauty of nature or activate my senses to my surroundings. The decision is mine. Let me say that differently: I have the executive power to counteract grief with joy. I believe that God created me to experience joy. I believe that the soul, my soul, has an affinity for joy. My soul comes alive when I experience joy. I also believe that joy is the golden inlays, the kintsugi effect, of healing the fractured parts of my soul following the death of a loved one. Kintsugi does not restore the old Terry, but creates a new Terry out of the fractured pieces of the old self with ethereal golden weld. Kintsugi does not smooth down the edges of the inlays. The inlays are rough and colorful to remind me that the broken can carry even more value than the original. The roughness of these invisible scars is a reminder I need of the healing that has taken place and the distance I have overcome since the cessation of one life and the beginning of my new life. I believe joy is one of the foundational elements of that weld. Joy can be layered and is one of the strongest elements to weld my broken self back together.

Doesn't every moment have a possible joy potential? There's always a chance that joy is just within my grasp in almost everything I do or experience in a day.

I do not have to circumscribe the globe like Juan Ponce de León in search of the fountain of youth to find joy. It is not elusive. It does not hide. It may be ever present, just within grasp. Can I see it?

I do not have to sit or study among the greatest academics to acquire a logical approach to joy. Joy is not derived from logical thinking. Joy may be understood by logic, but joy is something to be felt. It is an emotion. It is derived from feelings and more specifically derived from feelings of happiness. Can I feel it?

I do not need to take a rocket ship into space and extend myself to the far reaches of the ether to touch God to find joy. God provides joy free of admission to all. God himself is joy and the source of joy. He allows us to experience joy through nature and through the interconnectedness of friendships. Can I experience the joy God gives?

One does not have to dig miles into the Earth to uncover joy. Joy can be found in the bowels of the earth, but why dig when there is ample joy already available at a very superficial level? I probably threw all kinds of joy into the rock pile in the process of looking for the one mother lode of all joyful events. I must remember not to diminish the small aspects of joy always around me. Can I experience joy in its most elemental forms?

We don't have to spend a fortune of money to purchase joy. We do not have to cash in our life savings in the pursuit of joy. We do not have to work eighty hours a week through two different jobs to earn joy. It is available to all in copious amounts. It is a resource that will never be depleted. Can I relax enough to experience joyful events?

I believe joy can be learned. Like a muscle that is used repetitively hypertrophies, I believe that I can train myself to have a joyful outlook, lenses for happy events that germinate joy, the ability to absorb joy, and the awareness that it can center me.

My life changes for joy, and I make incremental changes toward joy that start weekly, then daily, then by the minute. It is a gradual on-ramp to the plane of joy. It functions in its own time frame and velocity.

Initially in my grief experience, there was no daylight at all. There was no happiness, and there was absolutely no joy. My heart and mind and soul were fractured, and they were not even communicating with each other. Joy seemed like the proverbial pot of gold at the end of the rainbow. Joy was so far removed from my life that even seeing people happy and joyful around me created spite within me. I hate to acknowledge that truth, but I have to call myself out.

Whether I didn't want to experience joy, whether I ran from joyful experiences, or whether I built a wall up against joy, God continued to place joy before me all along the path. Retrospectively, I recognize that he quietly put elements of joy all throughout the first year after Marlys's death. God was shadow writing these elements into my legacy. In retrospect, he even placed little flowers of joy within days of my wife's passing: rainbows on a driveway on a clear, sunny day and an underwater-swimming mallard duck. When nature goes against itself, heavenly powers are at work. I could not acknowledge these events as joyful during the moment; however, years removed from the trauma, I do recognize them as small buds of joy.

I was not thrown into a mountainous valley full of joyful wildflowers immediately after mortality slapped me in the face. It was a process. It was a maze. Many weeks there was no joy to be experienced. I wandered in an emotional desert. My emotions were as monochromatic as the elements my eyes could see. Some weeks I had to look for joy and search really hard for it. But out of those dark days and weeks and months, joy steadily presented itself more brightly and with more frequency. The darkness steadily receded, and time eroded through the thick layers of my grief and lament to allow more and more joy to be recognized and, moreover, felt.

Part of feeling joy for me is letting it roam through my mind off-leash, unhobbled, and unmuzzled.

The unmuzzled joy started within the safety of my four walls of the house or the four doors of my car. It was a personal transformation that had to take place in private places.

As time marched forward, joyful events and joyful experiences became more frequent. At this time, I am quietly but diligently searching for joy continuously. I started finding myself in places where joy could be found or where people were joyful. I attended concerts, walked the Lake Michigan shoreline in the winter, went to national parks, cooked steak on the grill, sang worship songs in church, and made connections with friends and family. Eventually, my joy came "off the leash," and it became public. I made my new self public.

I wish I could say that this was a straight-line trajectory from grief to joy, but it was a more twisted and convoluted process than I'd ever want to acknowledge. Many days I really don't know logically how I got to where I am other than the aspect of a common denominator: I pursued joy.

It is like a mural on a wall that was damaged and chipped and faded by the weather or by neglect. An artist comes along and re-creates a new mural on that wall over a period of time. But before fresh paint can be applied, the artist must power wash the wall, scrape smooth any rough places, and replace some of the mortar that's missing. This is the proper preparation necessary before a new image can be painted over the previous image. Once grief, sorrow, and lament struck, almost everything inside of me faded, blanched, fractured, or chipped. I had little semblance of my original character. Through this refining process the wall was being prepared for a new coat of paint, new vibrancy, and new opportunities to shine. Happiness is like the fresh paint going on the wall, the different colors and different layers of paint. Joy is the coalescence of all those colors into an image on that freshly cleaned wall. Joy is the meaning and purpose behind all those colors. It is what makes the painting pop, a smile to come to my face, or a tear to form as an appropriate response. God is the artist of my life, and his paint strokes are just starting to create new color and meaning in my life. This old wall is coming alive.

Now transformed by joy, I believe those of us who are grieving can re-create joy. As joy increases, grief recedes and softens. I must make the choice daily to find joy and to grasp it. I don't have to live in the haunts of grief forever.

Finding joy can be as easy as going out into a field and plucking wildflowers. Each day there are new blossoms to be plucked. Even though I picked them today, new buds await me the next morning. Whether it is a cloudy or sunny emotional day, joy remains ever present. Blossoms of joy endlessly bloom for enjoyment and picking.

THE MEMORY OF AN AUNT

Losing a Relative

Elyse Wood

I never met my Aunt Heather, but I know her. I know her in my grandpa's advocacy and my grandma's profound love. She is a picture, a guitar, a shoebox of homemade pins with silly sayings and cute drawings, a playbill with her name, a report card taped to the inside of my grandma's cupboard. She is a funny story, told over and over.

Her absence is a shape around which we all live, a shape that I never knew but hold in all my wonder. I wonder what my life would have been like with her in it. I wonder where my grandparents, my mom, my uncle, put their pain. I wonder how they carry it as they traverse the world she left. I wonder about her as I curl up on the floor with my nephews to draw with crayons; I wonder about her as I clap while my niece demonstrates her ballet from the stage of the coffee table. I wonder if, when I was a child, she would have drawn with me, clapped with me, lived in magic with me. I imagine her sitting next to me, her graceful hands guiding my child fingers across the neck of a guitar, showing me where to put pressure to evoke the desired note.

I wonder if my grandma would have painted with as much urgency, excavating that which cannot be found but in the furious strokes of watercolor brushes. I wonder if my grandpa's ache would have blossomed into a deep, warm, endless embrace of those whose ache was the same.

I wonder what her laugh was like. I wonder what her comfort would feel like to my fear. I wonder what it would feel like to be loved by her. I wonder what she would have taught me. I wonder if I would come to know intimately her depression and her joy. I wonder if she would feel less alone when I hugged her.

I wonder if any part of me would be able to draw out her essence into a ribbon so long it could wrap around her and keep her safe. I wonder.

three
Stories of Support

BREAKING THE BONDS

The Trauma of Perfection

Feral Yogi

Feral: Pronunciation /ˈferəl/ /ˈfɛrəl/ Adjective.
In a wild state, especially after escape from captivity or domestication*

As a child my wings were clipped, the adventure was washed from my feet as they were covered with black shiny shoes, my voice was hushed, and my once sharp claws were filed and blunted. I was handed a script, written in a voice that wasn't my own. A motion picture was placed in front of my eyes, flickering in endless repetition, replaying a script I was instructed to encode into my DNA so I could perform when asked—flawlessly on cue, just as if it were my own. I was a dancer in an endless performance, learning the perfect makeup strokes of a painted-on smile and the delicate footwork of each choreographed step in the production. Over time I learned to spin beautifully and rhythmically, just as programmed; but as the show progressed my knees lost their strength, and my turns became rapid, wild, and frantic. I became exasperated, spinning desperately until the soles of my shiny shoes wore through and my toes bled, my ankles sprained, and my intricately woven costume began to rip at the seams. Somewhere

---

* Based on the definition of "feral" in *The Oxford Pocket Dictionary of Current English*, Encyclopedia.com, last modified May 17, 2018, https://www.encyclopedia.com/humanities/dictionaries-thesauruses-pictures-and-press-releases/feral-0.

in the middle of this frantic dance of survival, my steps missed their mark, and I forgot my lines; my knees buckled, and I fell to the ground. Somewhere in the silence of that space the haze lifted, and I realized I was dancing to the beat of another's song. As I rose to my feet, I understood that if I truly wanted to take the lead, I had to overcome the fear of falling, stopping it all, and the unpredictable reaction of a show-thirsty crowd. So, I unlaced my shiny shoes and walked off stage to clean my bloody wounds. As I pushed open the front doors of the theater, took my first breaths of fresh air, and bathed in the freedom of unmanufactured light, I looked around and saw I wasn't alone. There were former performers everywhere; the familiar scars on their feet spoke of the pain endured when they decided to stop spinning and walk out into the freedom of their own light.

This is a walking-out story and a walking-in story. It's not just rewording the script, but shredding it, burning it, and learning to dance among the ashes. This is derailing the film, escaping captivity, releasing fear, and finding power in the rocky-road journey. This is where captivity stops and freedom begins. Join me.

As I look back on my life, it's hard to delineate the exact moment I was formally cast in the play. Being raised as the daughter of a strict and traditional Baptist pastor, there was no shortage of King James Bible verses to learn, souls to "save," and appearances to maintain. You see, what many don't understand is that when you're the daughter of the church's number-one "superstar," it comes with expectations. Only dresses are allowed; you may never wear pants, and for heaven's sake, cover your "sinful" body from neck to ankle. There's Bible class every morning, church services four to five times a week, and chapel on Wednesdays. If you're late, you're guaranteed a glaring look from the pulpit that would send chills down even the most hardened warrior's spine. Apologies are made publicly in front of the familiar painted smiles of a self-righteous audience, and you must accept their prayerful outcries for your soul when you violate yet another unspoken gospel rule. You are to have no friends outside of the church or the parochial school where you are pumped full of "facts" (such as that men have one fewer rib than women) to validate a literal interpretation of what I now know to be Bible parables. You may only listen to religious music, sing only religious songs, forgo dancing, and attend functions sanctioned by the church. You come early, you stay late, and most importantly you show no weakness or misalignment with the family image that took so long to curate. If the pressure gets to be too much or the weight of life becomes too heavy, you must pray, take your burdens to God, or consult with the pastor (which happened to be my dad) because outside counsel, such as receiving formal psychological therapy, was disallowed by the church, for *no* burden is too great to be solved by the institution of the cross.

This was the foundation, the stage on which I learned the steps of my first choreographed turns, memorized the words of the script, and began spinning to the notes of a song written for me long ago. We don't dare say it out loud, but it's indoctrination, and it's common throughout the country as well as in circles where I was raised. It works beautifully to create an obedient and fear-filled audience, but they messed up and miscast me—it wasn't a role I was destined to play.

When tragedy struck our family at a church event, leaving my mother paralyzed, unable to form coherent sentences from the resulting brain injuries, and psychologically traumatized beyond recognition, you'd think our world would stop spinning, but it only picked up the pace.

As life was rearranged, ramps installed, and doorways widened on our home, we never talked about the pain that each member of my family suffered in silence. This wasn't the first time tragedy struck our home, and it wouldn't be the last, but it was a catalyst that enabled me to see the danger of the dance we were desperately trying to perform. Since our religion didn't allow for psychological help or therapy of any kind, our family collectively (and individually) entered an irreversible downward spiral. From opioids and suicide attempts to neglect, abuse, drug raids, and gun violence, everything was hidden behind closed doors as we continued painting on our artificial smiles, assuming position, and stepping on stage to perform the dance the audience paid to see.

Despite our best efforts, our suffering must have been obvious, as the church "family" became uncomfortable and began side-stepping our family to avoid the evident pain behind our attempted smiles. Over time I began to see through the smoke screen of their contingent adoration. I dropped out of religious school and threw myself into every club, sport, and secular learning opportunity I could find. Since my homelife was in a constant state of free fall, I found solace in the concrete. I loved the structure expressed by the language of numbers, in tangible laws, in daily schedules, and in this new world of facts previously unopened to me. At night I took care of my mother and younger siblings while teaching myself math and science to catch up to my newfound peers. I expanded my worldview over and over again, without slowing down to realize this new way of life violated every religious rule previously encoded in my DNA. I began questioning religious norms and presented alternative perspectives to the indoctrination of their rhetoric. As a result, church leadership took a vote and decided that I would be shunned from interaction with my peers—it devastated my world. My soul felt as if it broke into a million pieces as the relationships with my church family crumbled along with the foundation of my collapsing homelife. But somewhere in the middle of the rubble, as the debris of my once beautiful stage came tumbling down, I saw a stream of light flood in from the outside world. It was then I realized I had a choice: I could fear the unknown, make it all go away, publicly apologize for my "blasphemy and disrespect," and conform to the "agreed upon" rules of the religious game, or I could be brave.

I could stop spinning.

I could break free.

So I threw my shoes off, and out the doors I ran.

We are all domesticated or systematically programmed, and we subject ourselves to conformity throughout life. Like performing a choreographed dance, at a young age we are stripped of our primal rhythm and programmed to "stand up straight," be a "good" girl or boy, and "fall in line." We don't know any better, so we unwittingly trade our bare feet for the allure of shiny shoes and exchange the taste of the sunlight for the familiar smell of chalkboard conformity. We do this for a variety of reasons—to appease our family, friends, social circles, or the silent demands of a faceless crowd. While some domestications ultimately serve and lead to greater safety in navigating the world (such as looking both ways before you cross the street), others enslave us and hold us hostage to their uncompromising demands. Over time we begin to identify with these demands; brainwashed, we call them our own. Whether or not we realize it, we are the captors, we are the prisoners, and we are the cage. The weapon harnessed against us, standing guard at the door, and keeping us enslaved? Fear.

Fear: it may sting, but let the word linger, and don't avert your gaze. Feel it. Look it in the eye and say its name out loud, for it has whispered yours a thousand times. It doesn't tremble or retreat when it locks its sights on you, so be brave and own it. Whether it's backlash from violating social expectations, fear of judgment, or stories of perceived failures we refuse to release, we have all been held captive by the paralyzing chokehold of fear.

It's the invisible force that keeps us stuck, weighted down, or disillusioned. Fear is hard to catch and even harder to evade, as it shapeshifts through time and space, taking on a million names, a million faces, and a million forms. But if you choose to stop and remove the mask of this faceless predator, you'll see it always answers to the same name—*fear*.

Perhaps it's fear of grieving or fear of letting go, fear of being swallowed by the enormity of your emotions or fear of truly being seen; maybe it is fear of pain, of rejection, of failure, of taking responsibility, of not being "good enough," or of being shunned and left all alone. Maybe it's fear of saying goodbye and moving forward or going against the grain and raising your voice. You may feel fear of the possibility of chaos, disapproval, uncertainty, betrayal, or death.

As you can see, there is truly no shortage of ways fear weaves its way into the fabric of our psyche and everyday lives. But one thing is imperative for you to understand: despite its attempts to make you feel isolated in your suffering, you are not alone, for this fear is shared collectively among the whole. It may be disguised, masked beneath different experiences, traumas, and expectations, but it always plays the same confining role, attempting to stand in your way of stepping out into the power of truly living your life (in all its pain, beauty, colors, and seasons).

For as much as we crave the color of a new sunrise, fear chains us to replaying the sunsets and storms of the past. It prohibits us from stepping forward, evolving, forging a new path, and tasting the fresh sunshine of life outside the script.

Don't worry; as strong (nefarious, endless, or dark) as fear may feel, *you* are infinitely more powerful than it could ever dream of becoming, for you have been gifted the secret weapon of choice. Every time you refuse to shy away and reclaim the might of your voice, you disempower fear—and it all starts by stopping.

It starts by slowing down and refusing to participate in the pattern of the dance. It's recognizing the way that fear has woven itself into your life and stripping it of control by power-thrusting it into the light of awareness. It's refusing to bow to the demands of a fear-based mindset or show-thirsty crowd. It's looking at your past, acknowledging your scars, engaging your trauma, applying a heaping portion of love to those soul-wrenching defeats, and tending gently to your openly infected wounds. It's unlocking the doors, escaping mental captivity, and releasing the trauma bond we have with society's expectations. It's calling fear out by name and day by day gaining insight from the scars you gained in surviving the battle.

It's you.

It's me.

It's *we*, healing ourselves and the world, by standing in the truth of who we are, being brave enough to learn a new dance, and sharing the golden struggle of our individual hero's tales. For every time we share our story, we empower others to walk out of a crumbling theater, take a fresh breath of air, and feel the freedom of their own unmanufactured light.

There is power in your story, so stop spinning and start healing today by asking yourself: *What stories, beliefs, thoughts, or patterns do I hold that keep me feeling stuck, weighted down, or confined?*

What would I be able to do differently in my life, if I allowed myself to choose a different, more empowering story, belief, pattern, or perspective?

What's one small thing I can do and desire to do today to begin to take new steps forward?

For extra oomph, list three ways you've shown resilience or strength in the face of these adversities in the past. Don't be shy. You're a powerful being—own it!

NOT SO PICTURE-PERFECT

The Trauma of Addiction

Cassandra Wilfore

One might call this a story of star-crossed lovers—two people with a love so deep that everything else faded out of existence while they were in the eyes of each other. But where there is light there is darkness, and so was the case with this tragic love story.

It all began one summer day in West Michigan. Abigail was working as a waitress at a local pub where, on this particular night, they were hosting a Hawaiian-themed party. One of her coworkers, Emma, had a special guest in town whom she had invited to join— her brother, Sam.

Abigail was not one to fall head over heels and lose all control. In fact, she was notorious for having the guys lining up for her attention without much luck. Sam was different. It was love at first sight, and she knew in her heart right then and there that there was something very special between them. It was a powerful infatuation, the kind of love that makes you give up your life, quit school temporarily, and move to another country just to be by this person's side. And that is what she did.

Sam carried with him a story of hope and inspiration in his success of overcoming negative patterns and turning his life's purpose toward that of a better path. He was a high-school dropout who was

Names of individuals have been changed for anonymity.

arrested at age seventeen for stealing booze. After seeing his son on the cusp of a jail sentence, Sam's father convinced the judge to grant permission for Sam to instead attend a "spiritual boot camp rehab" in Florida. Sam stayed at the Florida center for five months, where he met Sister Alessia, who convinced him to move to Italy to help manage a clinic for heroin addicts. He lived in Italy doing this for about a year before he was then again convinced to move, this time to the Dominican Republic to help at an orphanage. It was during a visit home from the Dominican Republic that the eyes of Sam and Abby connected, and life would never be the same.

That short introductory visit was enough to immobilize Abby with Sam's departure. She knew her life was meant to be by his side, and it wasn't long before she decided to take a break from college and move down to the Dominican Republic, where she could live her life next to him. Together they spent a year on the island before they made their way back to Michigan to enroll back in school and start a life together.

Following Sam's earning his GED, both Abby and Sam enrolled in a local college, from which they both graduated. During this time, Sam proposed, and Abby became pregnant with their first child, who was an unexpected miracle to say the least. Sam went on to study law for three years while Abby, with her double major in finance and marketing, served as the breadwinner. They got married and had their second child. Sam passed the bar and began excelling in his legal career, first in the public defender's office and then in private-practice opportunities. Abby went on to raise her beautiful family, build a gorgeous home, and become a very successful realtor.

On the outside, their life together was a picture-perfect painting of the most perfect love story—a journey from rags to riches, from dust to triumph. But as with all stories, you should never judge a book by its cover. As a teen, Sam was labeled as a criminal. What was perhaps overlooked was the role that addiction may have had in all his struggles and transgressions. It is not uncommon for recovering addicts to work in rehab facilities, as Sam did while in Italy. It is a motivating distraction that gives purpose and meaning to life in the absence of an addictive substance. These people are called "recovering addicts" and not "recovered addicts" for a reason. Addiction is a lifelong battle, one that cannot just be written off as recovered and over. A true addict will suffer from the disease, or work to fight the disease, for the course of their whole life.

Sam's addiction, his disease, was always a part of him. Despite the good in him, he carried with him these demons, which he could never seem to shake. However, Abby's love for him was a force not willing to cease. She wanted so badly to fix him, as it was only the addiction that stood in the way of their picture-perfect fairy-tale life.

That's the essence of a fifteen-year fight with addiction that their relationship endured. Sam was sober when they met, but it wasn't long before a new obsession would take control and Abby would fight to hold on and fix him. Sobriety from these addictions, or obsessions, would follow because of some drastic measures such as rehab, usually after a destructive event, such as an overdose. And the cycle would start again; so, on and on it went. First it was alcohol, which turned into prescription drugs. From the prescription drugs it went to heroin, cocaine, and meth. All surprisingly were well hidden under the glitter and fame of the public eye. Only those closest to Abby and Sam knew the truth, and even the intensity of that truth was diluted to a degree because of Abby's image-protection methods.

Abby did work hard to make sure that what others saw from the outside was the picture-perfect image she saw, if only in the absence of the addiction. And she did a damn good job with that. She spent fifteen years in a state of hyperalertness, ready at any moment to step in to save Sam, protect their kids, and protect their image. Meanwhile, Sam would continue to ride the roller coaster of addiction through relapse and recovery, over and over again. "This is the last time I will allow him to do this, I promise," was her motto. But it never was. Not until the summer of 2016.

Sam was running for elected office when during his campaign he slipped back into his addictions. At first it was alcohol. When Abby discovered it, she hit a boiling point. She threatened divorce seriously if he didn't go to rehab. He refused and did nothing to repair the relationship. He didn't return home. She was left with no choice in her heartbreak but to move forward with the divorce. It was never what she wanted. She had done everything in her power to support him and stand by him through the hard times. But she knew she could not continue trying to save and rehabilitate Sam alone. She loved Sam but could not tolerate the daily struggles he put her through.

Sam rejected Abby's pleas for therapy and rehabilitation. He rejected her and their marriage in that decision. At this point he had become a victim of the disease, and nothing else mattered more. With no signs of improvement, neither in Sam's condition nor in their relationship, Abby moved herself and their kids in with her mother and stepfather.

But Sam would not bow to the control of her decisions for his family. He quickly turned the tables to threaten Abby's sanity, safety, and life. He threatened her in her decisions, saying he would make sure the whole world thought she was crazy and she would never see her kids again. This may sound like an empty threat, but because Sam was a successful attorney with many wealthy and influential connections on his side, she felt powerless. He began his articulated attack. He placed a restraining order on her, preventing her from returning to her own home. Then he hired people to follow her around and spy on her, her family, and her best friend. He traced every move she made, and she felt trapped. Not only did these hired "spies" follow her around, but they even put her and her loved ones in danger. One drove straight at her mother while she was walking her dog, so she had to dive out of the way for safety. Meanwhile, threatening phone calls persisted day in and day out. And if it wasn't threats being sent, it was flowers, but with no wish for reconciliation. He stopped paying their bills and went into a hole. Abby felt she had lost all control of the situation.

If the pain from the separation, harassment, and abuse wasn't enough, then came the public shame. While they were aware of his relapse into alcohol, Abby and the family were not aware Sam was doing drugs again until his public overdose happened, when his heroin overdose hit the news and TV stations. Yet, even in the public shame, Abby rushed to the hospital to be by his side. But even there he rejected her once again, enforcing the baseless restraining order that he had in place to punish her and sending her to jail. It was devastating to Abby to have all this in the public eye, and she was embarrassed to go outside. She had been put high on a pedestal during Sam's campaign and was now torn down with shame from his addictions. While the divorce wasn't final, she quickly changed her last name personally and on her real-estate signs for her business.

Her son was embarrassed to go back to school. At this point, the momentum of the destruction from Sam's addictions was so powerful, it seemed that nothing could stop it or reverse it. The divorce process continued forward despite their love.

Even in his faults, Abby loved Sam with all her heart. And in my love for her I chose to love him, too, even when I saw the pain he was causing. It was her life and her choice to be with him, not mine. She knew his demons, and she chose to love anyway. She had so much hope and faith, but it was not in her control. She wanted to believe she was enough for him and could fix his brokenness, but that decision was not with her; that's a hard pill to swallow in love.

In the end, the abuse from addiction destroyed Abby. In 2017, she chose to end the pain and suffering when she fell to her death from the top of a parking structure. One and a half years later, the addiction itself also destroyed Sam with a fatal overdose. And now their beautiful children, pieces of the memory of a love they once shared, are all that's left of this tragic love story. And I'm broken. All who loved them are left broken and feeling powerless. Addiction broke us all.

This is the short version of a very long story of abuse at the hands of addiction that took the life of one of the world's most beautiful souls, my best friend, Abigail. I get frustrated when people label suicide as mental illness. Not because it's not, but because the term "mental illness" itself has a stigma with the majority of society as something of a disease—as if there were no causes and as if there is no one else responsible but the person suffering. And then you have your culprit to blame, and you can move on from the discussion—as if it can't happen to you. But the truth is, there is a very fine line between a stable, happy person and one who is painfully suffering. It's a matter of a decision, a mistake, a moment. Most of us experience suffering, and most of us suffer in silence. Addiction is a killer. It is a master abuser to all those it touches—not just the addict. I dare to say that addiction painfully abuses the people who love the addict even more. But I only know one side personally.

AN UNEXPECTED JOURNEY

The Trauma of Addiction and Divorce

Jennifer Feuerstein

Building a backbone of steel doesn't happen when life goes according to plan. Rather, it comes about when the easy life you anticipated becomes so hard that the resolve inside of you is molded into metal. I had a picture-perfect life invented for myself. But the idyllic fairy tale I dreamed up was rewritten by a series of tragedies.

I lived a quiet, upscale, suburban life as a wife and mother home-schooling, cooking from scratch, and volunteering for church. Two years after my son was born, my husband and I wanted more children. With the ease of our first, we had no reason to believe we'd have problems. But for the next seven years, we mourned in anguish the loss of five pregnancies, the first four to miscarriage and the last to an ectopic pregnancy resulting in emergency surgery to save my life. It was a harrowing time. And then, unexpectedly, we conceived and welcomed our second son, followed by a precious daughter two years after him.

During the years of infertility, I was blinded by my own grief and didn't see my husband deteriorate into alcoholism. We finally had the children we yearned for, and yet the insidious disease crept in and began to destroy the life we had built together. Our home was turned upside down by the evil of alcoholism that evolved into chaos of other addictions. When the toxic environment became too unbearable and unsafe, I packed up my three children (ages eleven, three, and one) and moved out on the fly. It was a frantic escape with an army of volunteers moving us while my husband was away.

I fell off the pedestal of my suburban lifestyle. Life shifted from the anguish of infertility to the devastation of alcoholism and divorce. I lost my beautiful home and lived in my mom's basement until I could recover financially. I absorbed a mountain of debt from the divorce and ended up on food stamps and financial assistance. I lost my marital status as a wife and became a divorced woman. I lost my vocation as a stay-at-home mom and became a single working parent—taking a job I had no experience in, within an industry I had no knowledge of. I mourned the life I once had. I felt like Job in the Bible, stripped of nearly everything.

I was awarded full physical and legal custody of my children. I now had the full weight of parenting on my shoulders alone. I was raising my children as a "solo parent," which is very different from single parenting. Single parents co-parent and likely receive stable child support or every other weekend off to get a break. They might get help with making decisions about education or discipline or conflict resolution. But as a solo parent you're flying alone. There is no other parent providing support. I struggled with the limitations of playing both mom and dad to my kids. But I constantly prayed that where I left off, God would pick up. I simply felt inadequate not being able to give them what a father could.

As time passed, my perseverance and God's goodness allowed me to dig myself out of debt and buy a home. I climbed my way up the career ladder, carrying my kids with me, to enjoy a stable financial life. I took vacations, paid for sports for my kids, and dined out with friends. I had recovered financially and emotionally and was ready to find love again and a father figure for my kids.

Seven years after my divorce I met a man who stepped into our lives. But I was naive and didn't know other types of dangerous men existed. I didn't know the evil of narcissism.

I was quickly swept off my feet. I bought into all the shallow promises of the dream life he sold me on. I married him without knowing he was a covert narcissist lingering beneath the surface of incredible (false) charm. As soon as we returned from our honeymoon, the emotional abuse began. I was subjected to gaslighting, verbal berating, and insidious lies and manipulation. Slowly I lost my sparkle. I filed for divorce exactly two years after we were married. My world was rocked once again. It was soul-crushing. I wanted nothing more than a happy marriage with a family portrait that included two parents, not just one. I wanted a co-partner in life.

After the second divorce, God placed people in my path whom I was able to counsel. I shared empathy and deep understanding because of the painful experiences I endured. One mom moved in with me temporarily to heal from her unhealthy marriage, and I walked side by side with three others who were escaping their own abusive marriages. I couldn't have helped these friends had I not walked this path myself. And while it was traumatic, I wouldn't change it because of the ways I've ministered to others.

I soon regained my sparkle and rebuilt my life once again. I healed and became more content in life than ever before. It was letting go of my grip on what life was supposed to be that led me to find happiness again.

I honor my wounds because they are what make me sacred and have given me strength. I'm proud of the woman I've become, and I don't think of myself as a victim. My journey is what has shaped me into the person I am. I barely recognize the woman I once was, because I've grown so much. In the midst of trauma, it's hard to see the way out, but time does heal our wounds. And we do emerge from the pain. I've been a solo parent for sixteen years; my two boys have now flown the coop, and my daughter is right behind them. God has also brought a wonderful, kind, loving man into my life. We are engaged and I'm excited to build a future with him in this next season as an empty nester. I have a blessed life despite the tragedies I've experienced.

I tell my kids, "Life won't go according to plan. The sooner you accept this, the easier life becomes." I have a story that's far different from the one I was writing for my life. I've earned a strong backbone, a soft heart, and a life that is far from perfect, but lovely, nonetheless. My faith has carried me. My experiences have carried others. My life mantra is "beauty from ashes" because time and again God has cleaned up my messes and restored my life to be beautiful. And he's not done writing my story.

THE POWER OF FORGIVENESS

The Trauma of Loss

Diane Neas

When I was asked if I would like to share a piece of my writing for this book, I was both honored and thrilled. I write constantly, but when I considered what to write about for this chapter, I suddenly became anxious. *Will my words sound hollow? My thoughts, silly? Do my experiences matter to anyone but me? Is anything I write worthy of being put into print?* Shaking these nagging doubts from my head, I've settled on the one fact that has kept me going in the sixteen years since my daughter was killed: I get to talk about my Becca.

On January 21, 2007, my daughter was killed at approximately 2:10 a.m. on a dark, cold stretch of highway just outside the city where we lived. Her life was taken by a drunk driver. I made it to the crash scene within an hour of when she died. When I learned the driver had survived, I was enraged. I wished him dead. I had hoped the injuries he'd sustained, which were serious from what the police officers told me, would end up being fatal. They weren't.

Before I continue with the time after her death, let me share with you who she was in life. Becca was a twenty-three-year-old college student studying early childhood education at Grand Valley State University in Allendale, Michigan. She was a nanny to a little boy. To her twin brothers, she was the world; she was their Sissy. Becca was my firstborn, my only daughter. My three children were my entire world and my reason for living. She was loud and funny, ethical to the core. She was the first to stand up and fight for the underdog. Beautiful, hardheaded, with a heart of gold, Becca was everything I wish I could have been as a young woman. I knew she was going to make the world a better place.

Upon her death my world went dark. It was as if a nuclear bomb had detonated and left my surroundings unrecognizable. When I realized this was going to be my new life forever, I didn't want to be here anymore. The anguish one experiences with the death of a child is unimaginable, indescribable. I felt I had no reason to exist for one more day.

But exist I did. Day after day the years stacked up. The heartache grew heavier. My desire to remain in the world didn't change much either way. I went through the motions, poorly.

My life was a mess. I drank too much red wine. I hated families that were intact. I didn't take care of the two remaining children that I had, my twins, Gabriel and Matthew. In truth part of me didn't believe I deserved to have them because I wasn't able to keep my daughter alive. The biggest regret of my life is the way I was a mother to them in the time after Becca's death. The boys did not get the mother that Becca had while she was growing up. They deserved so much more from me, and I am forever grateful that, as adults, they have forgiven me.

Today, my life is so different from what it was a decade ago. It all started to change when I made the decision to forgive the driver who killed my child. This wasn't an easy place to get to, but when I did, I couldn't believe I hadn't arrived there sooner. Forgiveness, for me, was the most healing thing I could do to help myself have a better life, the life I know my daughter would want me to have.

I had to fight the idea, which I held firmly and sometimes still revisit, that forgiving her killer somehow said I was okay with what had happened—that I didn't love her as much as I thought I did because I could forgive the person who ended her life. What kind of mother does that? At first even considering it made me feel like a monster.

My daughter was in the same car as the drunk driver. She'd given away her keys and accepted a ride from him at the urging of his cousin. The drunk-driving crash was his second incident involving alcohol and being behind the wheel. He should not have been driving. He should not have been drinking. His choices led to my child dying on that January night.

One single thought kept creeping into my head: *What if it had been my child who killed someone by making a very bad choice? Would I want my child to suffer for the rest of their life for a poor decision? Would they deserve to be punished for the next sixty years? Did they need to lose their life as well?* I had to answer the question with no. I would hope that someone could extend grace and forgiveness to my child. If I wanted that for my own child, how could I not extend it to another's? I had no choice but to forgive him. As I said, it took a long time to get to this point, so please do not give me too much credit for being a good person.

There was a lot I had to consider upon making my decision about whether to tell him about my forgiveness. He'd been released from prison after serving four years. What if, upon his release, he'd gone back to living life the way he had been? I could find out he wasn't sorry for what he did. He could tell me he didn't need any forgiveness. At worst, he could tell me to go to hell. How would I handle that? Rescind my forgiveness? Was I better off having forgiven him in silence and not taken the chance of jeopardizing my healing by a negative reaction from him? Pondering all of this, I had to accept that such a negative response might truly be his reaction and I had to be okay with that. That is when it clicked that forgiveness was for me. As cliché as that sounds, it's true.

Yet, I hoped that knowing of my forgiveness would help him heal, as well. Maybe, being a little full of myself, I thought it could help ease his guilt if the mother of the woman he killed told him she had forgiven him. However it was going to turn out, I finally decided it was time to put action behind my decision.

I wrote a simple letter. It said that he and I were bound together by the same beautiful soul. I expressed my forgiveness and extended an invitation to meet face-to-face and talk. My cousin put the letter in the mail for me, and I waited. A few weeks later there was an envelope in the mail with his name written on the sender's place. I don't remember the order of texts, phone calls, or emails, but eventually we set a time and met. We met at a restaurant. Both of us brought along support. Upon seeing him, I cried and opened my arms for him. He cried as I held him. The first meeting lasted a little over an hour, and we just talked from the heart.

Since then, we've stayed in touch, talking often, meeting up for coffee now and then. I care about what happens to him. I am a mother. I must. He is a good man who made a bad choice that cost my daughter her life, but that isn't all he is.

This meeting was a turning point for me. I was lighter. I no longer felt as if the world owed me anything. I accepted that the crash had happened, and Becca was not coming back. I understood that accepting this did not mean I didn't love her. Nor did it mean I condoned his actions. That, in itself, was freeing for my soul. With my soul lightened I was able to begin to engage in life in a positive way again! I also found out that healing, for me, comes in the service of others.

After such an incredible loss, one must find a purpose in living. I found mine in the care of animals, both domestic and wild. Animals are vulnerable and need a voice. I have a lot to say, I've realized. There is healing in helping others heal. I saw this firsthand in my relationship with the driver, and I see it daily as I care for people's pets at my job and in the wildlife I am called to rescue.

Last year I had no idea where my life was truly headed. In the past six months, I've been directed toward a volunteer trip to Sicily, where I will help at a street-dog rescue facility. I am excited to see how my healing deepens and widens when I am in a completely different environment. I am thrilled to be able to be of service.

I will keep healing every day.

THE FALL THAT CHANGED MY LIFE

The Trauma of Physical Pain

Christian Raguse

After high school in Western Michigan, I decided to make the leap north to the Upper Peninsula of the Great Lakes state, known for its pristine wilderness, beaches, and companionship. I thought that pursuing a degree in geological engineering at Michigan Tech would grant me access through the best, most practical door to the rest of my life.

Engineering is sometimes looked upon as a "noble" field to enter for any wide-eyed high school graduate. The formula is simple: engineers observe human life as well as our methods of invention, production, and consumption, with the goal of bettering the process and results for the generations to come. Oftentimes, people turn to engineers for their critical thinking skills when it comes time for humanity to face some of our most deeply rooted challenges, politics aside.

I was excited at first, considering I was living in the most mountainous region of the Midwest where I could continue to foster my passion for skiing and outdoor photography. At the same time, I would be making those at home proud of the prospective trajectory of my career.

The secret was, I never fell in love with engineering. I never fell in love with the meticulous process of deciphering chemical compounds and demanding derivatives. I was merely going through the motions in class, committing study guides to memory to escape the next midterm unscathed.

My passion lay in photography. I would spend all my free time outside of class either behind my camera at the local ski hill or behind my computer late at night discovering the nuances of photo editing.

My parents were proud; I had a quickly budding interest in something that would keep me out of trouble, while I maintained a passing grade in calculus three and mineralogy.

In my second year of engineering school, I fell ever more in love with the landscapes around me and the feel of my camera.

It was February 2017 when I went through the most traumatic ski accident of my life. A jump gone poorly at Mount Bohemia resulted in fractured C9 and C10 vertebrae, a crack in my skull, a relatively small hematoma in my brain, and a traumatic brain injury that would linger in effect for weeks if not a month or two.

Over the course of the night in the hospital, writhing in pain, I made a promise to myself: that my healing and recovery postincident must have direct correlation with the continual pursuit of experiences that would allow me to become a stronger, happier human being.

I had no option but to consider how fragile life and health can be. With such a severe pounding in my head and swelling across my face, I faced the reality that if I had not been wearing a helmet on that fateful day, I could have been strapped to a wheelchair in perpetuity.

I had taken so many blessings in my life for granted, and it took a severe brain injury for me to understand how quickly everything could be stripped from my grip. With a new perspective flowing through my veins, I knew I couldn't sit in the backseat any longer. All along, I had been watching the road unveil itself to me without my hands even on the wheel.

Within the next couple of weeks, as the swelling in my face subsided, I began to engage my brain with out-of-state college applications. I sent emails and messages on social media daily to professionals I had looked up to as a young photographer. Eagerly, I would scour the internet, trying my best to understand what such professionals had to go through to get where they were at the time.

I was free. I granted myself permission to leave behind what I knew and adjusted my vision toward what I wanted.

As the years since my injury have passed, I feel incredibly lucky to have worked on numerous photo projects with those I had looked up to for so long in the ski industry. I have taken trips out of the country to photograph my favorite professional skiers, have self-published two ski photography books, and have had my images displayed in some of the highest-regarded ski magazines in the world.

Above all, I have developed a newfound clarity for what's important for my well-being. I know when to say yes and when to say no. I know how and seek to honor myself and those around me every day.

I often wonder where the road could have turned if I never spent that long night in the hospital.

TIES THAT BIND

Shared Traumas

Maddie Woodrick

My family has always been proud of our connection with the Hemingway family. Yes, I'm talking about *the* Ernest Hemingway—literary and creative genius. My brother and I have always had a deep admiration for his work. My personal favorite is his short story "Hills Like White Elephants." I've always been inspired by his ability to use his words in a way that illustrates a story without saying anything about that story at all.

Ernest spent time in Horton Bay, Michigan, throughout the 1900s, the same area where my family had a cottage when I was a kid. He even wrote a short story called "Up in Michigan" as evidence of his stay there. Horton Bay resides on the shores of Lake Charlevoix and is located between the towns of Boyne City and Charlevoix. My happiest childhood memories took place in Horton Bay. When we were there my entire family was together: my dad, mom, brother, sister, and oftentimes our extended family. The most vivid memory I have of my dad while I was growing up took place in Horton Bay as well.

My dad was extremely passionate about fishing, and one morning he woke me up at the crack of dawn so I could embark on one of his adventures. I crawled out of my Pocahontas bed sheets, my mom dressed me in my favorite Scooby-Doo attire, and I waddled out to the dock with my dad, fishing gear in hand. I crawled into a tiny motorized boat, and we set out across the water that was as smooth as glass. Once we were at our desired location, we began fishing, and I curiously peeked my head over the boat to see the skeleton of a small sunken boat. I was bewildered and scared, but I was with my dad, so I knew I was safe. My dad and I returned to our cottage, and I was thrilled to show my mom the line of fish I was able to catch—or my dad caught. Regardless, we both caught some fish. My dad gutted them, and we ate them for dinner that night.

While I was growing up, I assumed that the story Hemingway wrote about his time in Northern Michigan reflected mine. I didn't think Hemingway blissfully set across Lake Charlevoix with his dad to fish, but I assumed "Up in Michigan" reflected a time of experiencing beautiful places and meeting beautiful people. One of the reasons I made that assumption is due to the friendship that my family, especially my brother, had with a man who ran a book and antique store called the Red Fox Inn. Jim was an incredible man who had a passion for books, but more specifically a passion for Ernest Hemingway. I remember Jim's kids, Ernest and Penny, would sometimes play on the beach with us or go sailing with my dad. Meanwhile, my brother would become lost in a slew of Hemingway books that Jim provided. He must have made a conscious effort for my brother not to come across "Up in Michigan," since my brother was not aware of the storyline until I initiated a conversation about it recently.

The storyline of "Up in Michigan" is far from a tale of beauty; instead it is a tale of pain and abuse. The story depicts a woman who is infatuated with a man. I had chills as Hemingway depicted the same general store my family would sit outside during Fourth of July parades, or the immense dirt road that leads to Lake Charlevoix—and, if you take a right turn, to my cottage. I had chills until the story took a devastating turn: that man took advantage of that woman and left her with nothing but feelings of confusion and violation. I also felt confused and violated after reading the story, so I turned to my brother and asked if there was anything else to the story. Was I missing the point? What was the underlying theme? He replied, "Do you think Hemingway is indifferent to sexual assault?" It was clear that we had both taken the same thing away from the story: Hemingway was either depicting his own experience or indifferent to the matter. I am still interested in anyone's interpretation of the short story, and quite frankly, I would love to hear a perspective that may enlighten me to something I could have missed.

Regardless of my disappointment after reading "Up in Michigan," it is impossible to disregard the connection that my family has continued to feel with the Hemingways. I definitely have a different perspective and opinion of Ernest after reading that story, but I am incredibly grateful for his granddaughter Mariel. In 2017, Mariel Hemingway came to Grand Rapids to speak at i understand's annual gala. She is beautiful and strong, and as an advocate for mental health while speaking out about suicide and addiction, she embodies everything I hope to become one day as a woman. She is the descendant of a legend but has established her own legacy as well. Mariel is very special to me because like me she is the youngest of a family that has suffered from various mental-health issues, and she has experienced a suicide not only in her extended family but in her immediate family as well.

As the youngest in this sort of family dynamic, we were both introduced to pain at a young age and had to watch helplessly as the people around us suffered. Mariel highlights these experiences in her book *Out Came the Sun*. I'll never forget when I first read that book; my jaw would drop at countless different experiences and challenges she described throughout her years as a child, teenager, and into adulthood. I screamed internally, "Finally! Finally!" I had found someone I could relate to, someone who had experienced the same exact emotional turmoil I did while I was growing up. These experiences made me feel isolated and even more reserved, as the painfully shy child I already was.

When I had the opportunity to thank Mariel for sharing her story after the i understand gala was over, we were both in tears. I cried even more when she wrote in my copy of *Out Came the Sun*, "Maddie, my own mountain daughter, stay in touch." I'm crying again while I write this. I have always believed that everything happens for a reason. I'm sure Mariel touched many other people when she spoke that night, but it almost felt as if she was meant to be there for me.

four
Stories of Healing

A CANDLE LIGHTS THE WAY

Healing through the Flame

Maria Zambrano Curtis

It was a cold January day in northern Florida, and I remember sitting in the car as we were driving to my new high school. Filled with emotions of excitement, fear, and sadness, I said goodbye to my dad in the parking lot. At the time, I was sixteen years old, an only child, and living without my parents for the first time. I thought that I would return home to Colombia in six months to start at the university to study chemical engineering. Well, it has been twenty-three years since that day, and I never went back to Colombia for an extended period of time. The United States became my home.

I spent the year in Florida. It was a magical time in my life, waterskiing and learning English. I felt free. I did not feel homesick, because I began to realize all the opportunities that were in front of me. I lived with my coach's family during this time; they had two kids, a boy and a girl, and I saw them as the siblings I never had. I was exposed to an entirely new environment, meeting a lot of people as well as experiencing a whole new language and culture.

That summer the days seemed to blend together, as each day was very similar to the next. Get up early in the hot Florida sun, put my bathing suit on, head down to the lake for the first ski run of the day—all while the Counting Crows blared in the background. That summer, based on a friend's recommendation, I applied to the University of Alabama. They had had a great waterskiing team for the last twenty years, and it was close to my coach's home, which was the only family I had in the United States at the time.

I was accepted to the chemical engineering program at the University of Alabama. I recall one of the most difficult conversations I have had with my parents. My plans had changed. I wanted to stay a little longer and get my education in the States. My mom cried. She never expected that I wouldn't return to Colombia after that first year. My dad asked me if that was truly what I wanted. I said yes. That yes changed my life. At the time, this was the biggest risk I had ever taken, and I began the journey I continue to be on today.

I moved to Tuscaloosa, Alabama, on a cold January afternoon in 2001. I had a red Ford Escort that I had packed with my skis and the few belongings I owned. That evening, it began to rain as I arrived. I parked in front of the engineering dorm I was assigned to and started planning how I would unload my car and get it up to my room without any help. I did it. My roommate was not there yet, and I had the whole room to myself. The room was big, and it had two twin beds. It was around nine p.m. as I started to unpack, and I realized I did not have any bed sheets. I placed a towel on top of the bed and fell asleep. It was the first time in the past year that I felt alone. The next day, I went to the registrar's office to complete some paperwork and asked where I could buy some food that I could cook in the microwave. I drove around campus for a while and could not believe how beautiful all the buildings were. The experience felt like it was right out of a movie. I bought a bed in a bag, a toaster, and some Lean Cuisine to keep me going until classes started.

As I navigated the Deep South with my heavy Colombian accent and without knowing many people, the next few weeks were the hardest. My ski coach and some of my teammates slowly started to reach out, and little by little I did not feel alone anymore. The next four years were the best years of my life up to that point. I had my first job, I met my future husband and my best friends, and I was able to graduate with honors with a degree that I loved.

The week after graduation, my longtime boyfriend and I broke up; he wanted to move to Los Angeles to pursue his dreams, and I was moving to Evansville, Indiana, to pursue mine. Once again, I found myself driving up to a whole new life. I had been accepted to General Electric's operations management leadership program. I felt grown up; I got an apartment, furniture, and a new car, all with my own money. After the adrenaline of the move faded, I felt alone again. I buried myself in my job and learned how to be a good engineer. My time in Evansville was one of the hardest up to that point, but filled with incredible personal and professional growth. A year and a half later, I graduated from the leadership program and got a full-time position in Montgomery, Alabama, at the plant where I had completed my internships during college. Montgomery felt a bit more familiar to me, as my best friend was there, as well as friends I had made during my time as an intern.

In March 2008 I reconnected with my college sweetheart, Eric. He was living in Los Angeles. After a year and a half trying a long-distance relationship, we needed to make a big decision. A long-distance relationship was no longer acceptable, and we needed to decide whether we could move to the same city, or perhaps it was time to move on. I remember Eric telling me that we were not going to get engaged before the move. We knew each other well, but some time had passed, and we needed to reconnect to see if we had a shot at a long-term partnership. I was terrified. I would be risking a job I loved to move to one of the biggest cities in the world, Los Angeles, with hopes that my relationship with my college sweetheart had a chance. I remember sitting on the tennis court of the apartments I was living in, having a long conversation with my dad about the pros and cons of the move. He asked me if I truly wanted to move, and then asked what I had to lose. Although I was very young, I was also tired of moving around. However, I wanted a family of my own and a home away from home.

While in the midst of a recession, in July 2009 I moved to Los Angeles. With my dog Bruce in the back seat, my mom and I drove from Alabama to Los Angeles in my little Honda Civic. It took us a week since we stopped in a few places along the way. I remember the trepidation I had. My emotions were mixed with sadness and excitement as I geared up for another big change in my life, the whole time wondering if I had made the right choice.

I started working at MillerCoors as a second-shift supervisor in the packaging department. There were many new interactions for me, and because this department was heavily unionized, sometimes relationships got to be a bit complex. I found myself in an awkward and somewhat lonely situation once again: a new city, few friends, a new job, a new industry, a new work schedule, and a new apartment. It was a big move that proved to be exceedingly difficult, even for someone who had done the wholesale-change thing a couple of times already. On November 12, 2009, Eric asked me to marry him, and I accepted. The year 2010 was a great year. I got married, got promoted a couple of times, and was looking forward to becoming a mother in the near future.

My firstborn son, Simon, arrived in December 2011, and my life continued to change dramatically. I now found myself navigating motherhood while simultaneously attempting to advance my professional career. Soon after Simon was born, Eric and I decided we were going to wait awhile to have another child. It did not seem wise to add another child since we had no family on the West Coast, and we were both pursuing careers of our own. A week after that decision, I found out I was pregnant, and Ana was born in October 2013. Being a working mother in a male-dominated field has been very hard but also very empowering.

In May 2016, we decided to relocate to Michigan, specifically where my husband is from in the small community of Ada near Grand Rapids. Our family goals shifted toward the pursuit of a more well-rounded family life for our kids. My husband's parents and sister lived in Ada, and the idea of Sunday dinners and holidays with family and plenty of kids felt exciting to us. The first three years of the transition to Grand Rapids were difficult. Yet again, I found myself navigating a new job, in a different industry, trying to make new friends, while learning how to be part of a bigger family unit.

At the end of 2019, my sister-in-law Linsey and I founded a candle company, LIMA—United by Love. Our passion project was not planned, but as soon as it started it became very personal and fulfilling. Linsey and I combined our names, our talents, and our passion to share love with others to unite, empower, and give back through our candles and gifts. In October 2020 Vonnie Woodrick reached out to us with the idea to create a candle for i understand. I met Vonnie for coffee, and my heart grew a bit bigger from that single interaction. We had an instant connection, perhaps fueled by a meaningful dime. As I introduced myself, she shared with me the mission of i understand and a bit of her personal story. She gifted me her first book, and I accepted her generous gift. I have not had much experience with mental-health issues. To be honest, my ignorance sometimes could have been perceived as insensitive. However, I went home that day and decided to read a few pages of the book. I took a seat at my kitchen table and started reading about Vonnie's story. I could not put the book down. I cried and felt emotions I had not felt very often. My eyes were wide open! I reflected on the beautiful soul I met earlier that day and the journey she shared in her book. I became energized and inspired by her courage to turn her sadness and pain into a beautiful work of love.

Since then, LIMA has supported i understand's mission by completing the Love Heals and Heart of Gold campaigns in February 2020 and February 2022, respectively. After several months of hard work and more than three thousand candles sold, we were able to donate over $20,000 to i understand. With these results, Linsey and I could not be more proud of our efforts. We saw the community rally around our company and i understand for this important cause. We heard many stories from new friends, and our understanding has continued to deepen.

My friendship with Vonnie through her book changed my life and opened my heart. Even though I have embraced significant change many times in my short forty years of life, I felt that those two hours at my kitchen counter reading Vonnie's story changed me the most. My heart was filled with empathy, and I found myself hungry to understand and to help. The truth is, change has been the only constant in my life, and perhaps it will continue to be. It has given me an incredible perspective and growth, and for that, I am forever grateful.

THE EYE OF THE STORM

Healing through Connections

Vonnie Woodrick

Days come and go. We experience fun days, happy days, sad days, some we cherish and some we want to forget. There are some days that play out for us in ways that have us questioning, Are our lives preplanned? Is serendipity real? Does everything happen for a reason?

Almost twenty years ago, two strangers unknowingly connected with different yet challenging experiences at the same place. This particular day set in motion a course of life for both of those strangers that had been unexpected and turbulent yet also filled with love and a newfound passion—a passion to make a difference. A friendship was bonded by the same day, November 4, 2003, but wasn't discovered until almost eighteen years later.

That frigid and dark November day was the most devastating day of my life. I entered the hospital with my husband, who was in the midst of losing his lifelong battle with anxiety and depression. I didn't know depression had a deadly side effect, one that was never talked about: suicide.

After four long days in the hospital, being a witness to my husband on a ventilator, with no movement other than a twitch of his eye, and waiting for test results to see whether brain damage had occurred, I sat in disbelief and devastation, questioning how we got there.

The hospital stay was the longest four days of my life. At times it still feels like yesterday, but at other times it feels like a dream. A very bad dream—a nightmare. I recall those days: each morning I would wake up and force myself to get ready and, for some reason, I wore his socks. His socks seemed comforting.

On November 8, 2003, I walked out of the hospital a widow, and my life, my good life, changed. Devastation, confusion, heartbreak, and shock followed, not just for days but for years. It took me ten years to be able to really talk about this loss and the effects it had on me and our three young children. Once I began to talk, others listened; they wanted to talk, too. Others had stories to share, and that sharing sparked something within me. I didn't just talk. I wanted to completely change how people spoke about mental/brain health illness and the effects those illnesses may have, and I wanted to re-write the narratives around these illnesses. I developed a passion—a passion for change.

In 2014, I created the nonprofit organization i understand. Our mission is to offer compassionate comfort and understanding to those who have lost a loved one to death by suicide or who live with a mental/brain health illness or pain.

Five years later, Ginger Zee, a chief meteorologist at ABC News, was the keynote speaker at our annual Celebration Dinner where we raised funds to support i understand's mission. I refer to Ginger as the "tornado through stigma" since her passion for creating awareness for mental health is evident when you listen to her speak or read her books, *Natural Disaster* and *A Little Closer to Home.**

Ginger and I connected, and she is someone I consider a friend, but it wasn't until she read my book *I Understand: Pain, Love, and Healing after Suicide* that we realized our experiences in life and our passion connected us.†

---

* Ginger Zee, *Natural Disaster: I Cover Them; I Am One* (Glendale, CA: Kingswell, 2017); *A Little Closer to Home: How I Found the Calm after the Storm* (New York: Hyperion Avenue, 2021).

† Vonnie Woodrick, *I Understand: Pain, Love, and Healing after Suicide* (Grand Rapids: Eerdmans, 2020).

This "tornado through stigma" now had an "eye of the storm."

It was September 11, 2020. I missed a phone call and then I received a message from Ginger:

To show how interconnected we all are, my heart sunk when reading your book November 8, 2003.

I left the hospital November 4, 2003, after my suicide attempt. Probably the same hospital you were at with Rob.*

I am sorry he didn't walk out too but I vow to keep sharing his story, your mission and keep helping all others with this illness.

Thank you again for your book.

I immediately called Ginger back to discover her tears were real and her emotions were raw, and we both agreed there was a bigger plan for us to connect, a connection that was cemented all because of a date that took place almost twenty years ago.

After taking a few days to process this serendipitous encounter, I sent Ginger this email:

I've thought so much these past couple days, about our conversation and our experience on November 4, 2003.

You walked out, a changed person. You went on to live such a beautiful life with so many wonderful unknowns and challenges along the way. You also became and have the power to be the "tornado through stigma" reducing judgment and stigma, finding the power in sharing stories, and are committed to making a difference.

Thank you for that.

You are changing lives while, I am sure, healing your own.

I walked in [to the hospital] on November 4, 2003, with my husband and walked out four days later without him. The journey

---

* Ginger was our hometown girl. We both grew up in West Michigan in neighboring towns.

has been long and difficult, yet I know Rob has been by my side every step of the way. Perhaps even having something to do with connecting us.

Rob gave me the gift of passion, a trait that I so admired in him. We share that passion. You . . . have touched my heart in so many ways. Love heals and comes from unexpected places. You are an unexpected place. Thank you for sharing you with me; more clarity came after our emotional conversation the other day. The journey continues to become clear.

It's crucial to continue to share our own stories without fear and judgment so others can know it is okay to live their lives openly and freely. Talking will not only change lives but perhaps even save a life or create a new bond that allows the realization of a bigger purpose.

Every minute of every day is a gift. The gifts we recognize along the way, the people who are brought to us throughout our journeys, lead us to where we are supposed to be. The storm is just beginning to brew. There is not only a "tornado through stigma" on a journey of wiping it out, but also an "eye of the storm" waiting to emerge.

HANDMADE

Healing through Art

Mara Carbines

I couldn't breathe. I wanted to; I knew I was supposed to. It was one of the small things everyone else wanted from me, but it was as if something was holding my breath. I didn't even really understand what was happening, though. Is an eight-year-old supposed to understand? Why in the world would an eight-year-old have such severe anxiety? I'm not sure I even believed it. The truth is that sometimes it's not *what* makes you have anxiety but the *way* your brain works. My father's job took him away from home a lot; so that separation every week would trigger anxiety, which led to worried thoughts that would make me think he was never coming back home. I had no real reason to believe this because my dad loves me and my mom so much and is the safest person I know. My mother also had some medical struggles (miscarriages, illnesses, and surgeries) that only heightened the feeling that my world wasn't secure. School would throw my brain off too. I saw classmates being so calm in class, not struggling with tests, reading books I could only dream of reading, and working through homework with ease, while I was sitting there with my mind racing, scared to death at times. Even though I was eight, I experienced feelings of being rejected, in danger, or insufficient, and I didn't have the rationale to pull myself out of it. I believed in God, but my worries would get in the way of my faith. The big problem is that I just went quiet, not knowing I needed help or even how to ask for help. I really have a fun, spunky personality when I'm not squashed by fear.

Finally, my mother saw glimpses of my struggle and started to get me therapy. It felt good that we were doing something, and I loved my therapist, but I hated going. I thought I had to be massively broken if I needed therapy. It was almost as if I couldn't take in the help fully. Then needing to take medicine for my brain made me feel even more off (and wow, finding the right medicine is not easy).

Creating art was just about the only thing that brought me peace and made me feel relaxed, comfortable, and accomplished. I'm talking big, arty messes and creations (from creating out in Dad's workshop, to sitting at Mom's sewing machine, to painting, baking, drawing, woodworking, anything). My mom and I would spend lots of time at our kitchen table drawing, coloring, painting—anything. We learned it was an effective coping method. Art class saved my life in school, and my mind was always thinking of things it could create. I would feel alive and not restricted with art. Why is it that learning art in school appears sometimes to be considered as lesser value than math or English; yet it can be a kid's true way to expand the mind?

Unfortunately, the "naughty toddler" in my brain (which is how my therapist would refer to worried thoughts) would nag at me and even make me stop short when I was creating—telling me it wasn't good enough, especially if it was different from what others were creating. But it was still my go-to every time to manage my anxiety (that and my massive stuffed-animal collection, but we don't need to talk about that). My parents stopped calling my savings a "college fund" and would call it my "art business fund." My mom did business strategy for a living, so she would always encourage me to dream of businesses. I think I helped her with some of her work from time to time.

Thankfully, I was finally tested in sixth grade (when I was still having trouble despite the therapy), and the test results clearly showed that I was dyslexic with both a visual and auditory processing issue. Do you know how excited I was to learn that there was something physically different about me and that a common side effect of my diagnosis was anxiety? Plus, dyslexia is actually common even though it wasn't as prevalent in my circles. It was a huge weight lifted. I now knew why my mind was somewhat normal, but that I also had a reason for thinking a little more "outside of the box" than others. The worried thoughts were wrong—I wasn't broken; I was made this way. I learned, though, that because of the way my brain works, anxiety will always be a constant for me, especially with triggers.

Two years later, in my eighth grade year, the COVID-19 pandemic stole all the fun "last moments" of being in junior high (class trip, sports, graduation, etc.). Then the unthinkable happened in the few months of summer: two incredible people in our lives committed suicide—two people I really looked up to. We ended up losing six people total in a short amount of time, and my whole family was hurting. My mind was so sad. Plus, I was starting a new school *online* (or in masks), only really knowing one other person—thank goodness she was my best friend. I'll tell you more about her later.

My mind was thrown off, anxiety was present in everyone, and I could feel it so much that my anxiety grew even more. My parents wanted to get me help, but unfortunately, everywhere was full. I did the only thing I knew to do: *create*—nonstop. I had learned about an organization in Detroit that helps people heal from trauma by creating purses and jewelry. I wondered if I could make jewelry to heal. I didn't know how to ask for help, but I put a couple of craft supplies in an online shopping cart, and thankfully my parents saw them and went for it, knowing I needed something. From that day forward, making earrings saved my life and my peace. Making earrings helped my mom and dad through their anxieties as well.

I created Star Shooters Handmade Goods where two-thirds of the profits go to mental-health organizations. I didn't know how to help others (how could I really when sometimes I don't always know how to help myself?), but I knew that helping others would also help me! So, now, one earring at a time, I heal my mind and put good out into the world. As I make earrings, I love my crazy mind and my crazy creations. The best ever is the community of amazing people who have connected with me and who support Star Shooters!

Remember that best friend I mentioned? She took a chance on me, choosing not to judge the things about me that seemed different. I love the slogan "Be the one for someone" because she was that one for me, and now I'm that one for others!

Now, I want everyone out there to know (especially amazing kids with anxiety, anyone with a learning disability, and anyone experiencing major, negative life triggers) that they are not alone, weird, rejected, or insufficient. I want everyone to know that they have someone who wants to know what is really going on. I used to be certain that I wasn't going to turn out to be much and that no one would want to know my real self, but now, I know differently and I'm already more than I believed I could be. Everyone deserves to shoot for the stars or at least to be able to hold their heads to look up.

I can't believe that I used to feel so different and broken. No one should feel that way. My favorite earrings to make are the ones that have something about them that's a little different or a little broken. I heard that there's a Japanese tradition to coat a crack in a dish with gold, and it makes the dish more valuable. They could easily throw out the dish when it's cracked, but instead, they turn it into something even greater. That inspires me so much.

I also make earrings that are mismatched, and I like watching the people who gravitate to them. I know that they must have the ability to appreciate differences and not feel threatened if everything isn't perfect. Whenever I meet someone who shares their mental-health journey, I become inspired to make jewelry for their story. A crazy thing is when I started making earrings, I didn't even wear them. I do now, though. I have never found a greater inspiration in my creating than being able to help others and myself.

I want our society to be more open to mental struggles, and I want people to know how to find healing methods. My method is art, but for others it may be running or telling jokes or sitting in the woods or getting help that shouldn't feel shameful. I want us to fight as hard for mental cures as we do for cures for breast cancer or heart disease.

Mental-health challenges are real. They are real in fabulous adults and cool kids. They are prevalent each day, especially with major life changes. It doesn't make anyone lesser. I will have anxiety my whole life, and I will be healthy, and I will *create* whenever I need or feel inspired! Please keep creating to find what heals for you, and know that you're definitely not alone!

A MOTHER'S TOUCH

Healing through Love

Sherry Homrich

Life feels beautifully ideal until it doesn't. You take pride in knowing that you understand your children until you don't. Words like *depression*, *bullying*, *worthless*, and *hopeless* become regular household words and feelings. Then the phone rings and there is chatter of theft, drugs, and deceit; your head and heart almost explode.

When this happened to me, I dropped to my knees and prayed. *What is happening?* We were all in a good space together, with so much genuine love, family unity, and faith. I prayed to see what was really happening in my home that had been our collective lovely respite. Now I understand that it had been concealed by lies, disguising the drug abuse. I prayed to know the truth, and guess what? God showed me what I needed to see, *not* what I wanted to see. Once I knew, I knew, though I did not yet fully understand that *addiction* was responsible. Drug use is a choice, right? Of course it is! Honestly, I always thought that if you had a drug problem, you should just *stop* doing drugs. Well, *addiction* is not a choice!

I'm the kind of person who is positive by nature and who is considered an open book. By that, I mean I've always felt we can learn something from one another, so why not be up front about our triumphs as well as our struggles? During this period of time, I began having trouble living as my true self; this led to shame creeping in.

My son's drug abuse was met by shock and disbelief by us and many who knew my son; it just didn't seem plausible. For a long time,

I truly didn't know the extent of the drug use or illegal activities. So, I began to research, stayed closer to home, kept a skeptical eye and ear out, and listened differently to try to become more aware, but he began to expertly conceal what he was engaging in. Nothing about the next several years was easy, joyful, or hopeful. Our home was charged with an unfamiliar feeling of angst. I barely understood the definition of *angst* before this. We watched our younger son retreat further into books and out into our workshop with headphones on so he would not have to hear or feel the tumultuous atmosphere that was our home. As we dealt with his older brother, we were not recognizing that our younger son was being bullied at school. There was so much anxiety, anger, and heartbreaking sadness on a daily basis. We pled, reasoned, discussed, cried, removed privileges, disciplined, and yelled, only to have it all fall on deaf ears. During this time we had so many counseling appointments, both individually and as a family. There was admittance into a mental-health facility, psychiatric appointments, court-appointed drug school, jail time, sobriety, and more drug use. Inside I was screaming, "Please just help me fix my son!"

My son is one of my favorite people on the planet; he was student of the month, he "lettered" in a varsity sport, and he is kind, thoughtful, and honest. I did not think he would ever do these things that people were saying he had done. Well, he did do all the things; he did do the horrible stuff and the drugs. We finally found out that his drug use was mind-blowingly worse than we had ever imagined. I became angry, impatient, joyless, and consumed with sadness, feeling a heaviness greater than I thought I could bear. I was unwilling to meet with friends or share the "whole" story with our extended family. Regardless of all the guidance we sought for our son, nothing seemed to be impactful enough to help him. I felt that *this* life was our new normal, *this* was how we would exist until something horrific happened or the elusive rock bottom came begging for our son.

After his second accidental overdose, I found myself sitting on my son's bedroom floor checking his chest for the gentle rise and fall of breathing while on the phone with doctors. I searched the internet for treatment centers, praying for Jesus to send me a message, a place where I could send him to save his life. My faith has been my rock, and so while scouring the internet, I noticed the constant message that kept reoccurring was *nature, nature*—the state of Utah popped up, repeatedly. Immediately I began researching what these treatment centers in Utah could offer my son. I became reenergized and overwhelmed with *hope*.

A week or so later, we sat down as a family to discuss my son's declaration, "If I don't leave home, I will die." Those words spoken aloud were the words I never wanted to hear, yet they were the words that needed to be said and felt. Our discussion of his leaving for Utah was not received well; he felt local counseling might work for him this time. Our younger son, who had initially told us he didn't want to participate in this discussion, finally chimed in and said, "What do you have to lose by leaving? Everything you're doing here is leading to your death." Our son left for Utah, by his own choice, three days later—he did not want to die! His therapy began in "the wild" of the mountains, living outdoors and learning practical survival skills all while getting intensive therapy. The only contact we had with him was through written letters, where the theme of "I want to live" was very prevalent. Meanwhile, we had weekly therapy appointments as well—damn, those are uncomfortable—pulling layers apart to begin a healing process after living in "fight" mode for too long.

Our son transitioned to other forms of therapy as he continued his path to healthier living, and we continued to see a mindset change, a passion to live! Several years have passed since that day, and our son still lives in Utah, choosing to stay after becoming sober. Our family is different now; we have a better understanding of why and how an addiction can begin. There have been setbacks on this newer path, but we are all wiser and, thankfully, less judgmental. We know that just because we love so very deeply, none of us can fix another person; they must do that work themselves. I joined a support group many years ago and still passively participate in the meetings; this group reiterated a healthier way to live when there is an addiction of a loved one. As a family we continue to talk openly about our mental health because our brains lack the optimal amounts of serotonin and dopamine, so we continue to research what is best with supplements and counseling for our family. This path isn't what we planned; it's been gut-wrenchingly brutal, but *hope*, however small, is always there, and shame holds no value or purpose in recovery. I am so thankful that we have a loving, supportive family that stuck by us as we got the assistance that has been truly lifesaving. With difficult changes and challenges come growth and wisdom. Laughter and joy return; they come with so much appreciation.

You may know our family, we may be your neighbors, but you did not know our whole story. So, if you're reading this, take a moment to be thankful that this isn't *your* story and *your* loved one. Remember that no one chooses to have an addiction, address your harsh judgment of others (and do better), and please show compassion and understanding to those who are living with an addiction.